Sweet
Sour
Bitter
Salty
Spicy
Umami
Temperature
Texture

Marriage of Flavours
Scott Pickett

Four seasons of beautifully balanced food

LANTERN

an imprint of
PENGUIN BOOKS

Photography by Dean Cambray

Spring   16

Summer   60

Autumn   104

Winter   148

Foreword

Scott Pickett is one hell of a cook. But then you probably knew that already. And like all great chefs, he's a man obsessed with food. Brutally honest, gloriously profane and eternally funny, Scotty is driven and fearsomely hardworking, hewn in the fiery furnaces of the old culinary regime. His technique is sublime, a delectable mix of classical French and modern, well, everything. With a palate to match. But it's his innate understanding of flavour and balance that makes his cooking so damned thrilling.

We first met a few years back, filming a show called *The Hotplate* – we were the Aussie chef and the English critic. After just 20 minutes, I felt like I'd known him forever. The hours were long, the shoot often gruelling, but whenever we had a spare moment we'd be off, in total thrall to our tummies, in search of Brisbane's finest ramen, Perth's best yum cha or Sydney's hottest new opening. Back in Melbourne, I'd sit at the bar at Estelle while Scotty worked, the sheer adrenalin of a busy service making his eyes gleam with delight. This is a man made for the kitchen. And there, armed with a book and a glass of wine, I'd happily eat my way through many of the dishes that appear in this book.

More recently, Scott opened Matilda, a paean to the art of cooking over coals. That Lakes Entrance baby octopus, the whole tiger flathead, those pickles . . . dear God, I could eat there forever. Once again, Scotty wanted a place that served up food of the very highest quality. No problems there – the critics raved, and the reservation lines rang (and still ring) red hot. Yet there's no pretence or pomposity to his cooking, no 'journeys', 'concepts' or 'philosophies'. Simply take the very finest seasonal ingredients, preferably local, and treat them with the respect they deserve. High art meets base pleasure. Which, for me, is the very heart and soul of Scotty's cooking.

The recipes in this book range across the globe from Italy, France and Greece to the Middle East, India and Japan. Plus Oz, of course. There are classics and old favourites alike, plus a whole load of Pickett specials. Divided into the four seasons, all share that essential freshness, flavour and lightness of touch that characterise his cooking. The notes on flavour profile are particularly enlightening.

Some of the recipes may look complicated but fear not: these are designed for the home kitchen and the home cook. I've only had the book for a few weeks and already it's fluttering with Post-it Notes and splattered from constant use. So, forget trend-driven, transient tomes about half-baked diets involving cave men and other such nonsense. *Marriage of Flavours* is a keeper, a book that will be as useful, relevant and much loved in half a century's time as it is now. At its heart is Scotty's blissfully simple mantra: 'Make it tasty.' Too bloody right, mate. Now, enough chat, it's time to start cooking. This book's an absolute beaut.

Tom Parker-Bowles

Introduction

One of the most difficult questions I'm asked is, 'which season is your favourite?', because, to be perfectly honest, I love them all – but for different reasons, of course.

Our summer barbecues at home, with heirloom tomatoes and zucchini salads, raw and cured seafood, summer berries and wonderful ripe cherries… Outdoor eating and cooking. Fun in the Aussie sun!

The wild pine mushrooms and quinces that let me know summer is ending and autumn is about to arrive. Pomegranates and prickly pears. The aniseed scent of new-season fennel, and the knobby little Jerusalem artichokes for my first warm soup of the year. Then being in the depths of winter and the slow-cooking that comes with it. Braised beef cheeks or the marrow inside *osso buco*. Roasted root vegetables and hot puddings that make me feel good inside, when the weather outside is anything but!

And then comes spring, just when my body needs it. The cooler months pass, and my need for spring greens really starts to go into overdrive. Broad beans and snowpeas, kale and sweetcorn, spring lamb; the wonderful green blush in the garden and warmth in the air make me feel better after the wind and rain have passed.

So, the seasons play an integral part in my cooking – and with that inevitably comes the flavours and their combinations. One of the things I'm often asked by keen home cooks is how to put together a dish or meal that's perfectly balanced. I suppose I've become known for how I bring together flavours and textures in my cooking, and it's something that can be incredibly fun. There are some tricks to it, which I'm going to share with you. When coming up with new menus for my restaurants – Matilda, Saint Crispin, Estelle and Pickett's Deli – it's the seasonal produce that's available and the flavours on offer that provide the jumping-off point. From there, it's all about bringing in ingredients both classic and a little unusual that will make the amazing Aussie produce really shine.

This book is about the food, the flavours and the dishes I like to cook for family and friends: it's my seasonal guide to constructing and designing balanced menus for you to cook at home. Some dishes are simple, and some not so – but those that require a little more are worth it, I promise you. I've given you a wide range of methods, interesting and familiar ingredients, and recipes that vary in their degree of difficulty. This will push some of you to try new things, and others to refine the techniques and knowledge that you already have.

I've also included some market tips and a chef's note for each recipe to help you along the way. These are just a few pointers that I've picked up on my own journey over twenty-five years in the kitchen. And not to forget that other element of a fantastic meal: something to drink with it! The starters, mains and desserts feature a suggestion for the perfect wine to harmonise with the different elements of the dish and make the whole experience even more enjoyable.

Flavour Pairing – and a Moment of Clarity

The first time I truly recognised and started to understand the marriage of flavours, I was twenty-three years old. I had been in a professional kitchen environment for more than eight years, but it took that long for the penny to drop. And, when it did, it really felt like a cloud had been lifted and I could see the light. Mind you, at this stage of my life I was already obsessed with food, yet I had been focussed solely on the technique; on the attention to detail that is required to 'cook a section' at the highest level. I was more focussed on cooking the perfect piece of fish or meat repeatedly than I was on what I was serving with it. That is, until I had a conversation I will never forget.

I was standing in the kitchen at The Square in London one afternoon, in between lunch and dinner service. All the other lads had gone on a break to the pub for a couple of hours, which was, to be fair, quite a rare occurrence. I had only been in the UK for about three months, and I wanted to impress my new boss, Phil Howard, so I stayed back to do a few more tasks. Phil loved it when the kitchen was pretty much empty, and he was working on new dishes for the menu. So, for the first time, it was just him and me.

After about half an hour I'd finished my work, so I offered to help Phil with the new dishes. That's when we really got chatting. The Square had received its second Michelin star just a couple of years prior, and had then moved from St James's to Mayfair. I wanted to know all about it. How did he do it? How did he get two stars? What made him different from everyone else? Where did his ideas come from? How fast did his Aston Martin DB9 really go? What drove him? So many questions and lots of answers; more than I expected. But the one that stuck out in my mind more than the others was probably the most simple and unexpected.

'Phil, how did you get two Michelin stars?' I asked. And his response was classic: 'I don't really know, they just happened to come along . . . I suppose people have always liked my flavour combinations, and we cook fuckin' tasty food'. It was that simple. A true revelation, and one of the greatest pieces of culinary wisdom ever shared with me.

Make it tasty.

Think about your flavour combinations.

The modern chef is constantly searching for innovative and different flavour combinations to set themselves apart from the pack but, as a home cook, unless you're truly skilled and have an extremely solid basis of pre- and post-modern cookery, I would suggest you stick to classic flavour combinations and give them your own little tweak. As Donovan Cooke once said, 'I don't reinvent the wheel, I just put new tyres on it.' I'd say that this is pretty accurate.

One of my simplest beliefs in life is that most things happen for a reason, and there's no exception in the culinary world. The seasons should drive flavour profiles and as they pretty much tend to be around us we just need to look. Follow nature's path and doors will open. Or think about classic combos you've seen on your travels, or in other countries.

Take duck and orange as an example. The orange can be substituted for any citrus or another form of acid to cut through the rich fattiness of the bird. Whether it's duck *à l'orange* or sweet-and-sour duck, the concept is the same.

Pork offers another perfect example. Pair it with apricots, apples, plums or sage, all classic flavour bases that you can explore.

Spring lamb just so happens to be at its prime when all the spring greens arrive. New season leeks, mint, parsley, baby peas, sugar snap, broad beans . . . Look no further, you have a perfect match.

Salmon and asparagus; add some dill, fennel, lemon and lime, and the dish is halfway there.

Beef and mushrooms – in a pie, as a side dish, or in a sauce. The earthiness of the 'shrooms is perfect with grass-fed beef. With some truffles, horseradish, parsley or thyme . . . The combinations are endless.

The versatile tomato has many friends that make it shine, too. Basil, onions, olive oil and pepper all make this humble ingredient sing with flavour. On that note, I like to use pepper more as a spice than as a necessary seasoning agent. Pepper is perfect – and a real non-negotiable – with certain things, such as eggs, potatoes, mushrooms and, of course, tomatoes.

Another thing that we need to take into account when constructing a dish is the balance. It needs texture for the perfect mouthfeel. It needs some acid, salt, a touch of bitterness, maybe a bit of creaminess, and something fresh or herbaceous to complete it.

It's the same when we cook multi-course menus. As chefs we look for 'a flow', which works really well at home too. If I'm cooking roast lamb, I might bring some mint into the courses that come before or after, or in a pea side dish with some creamy feta. And, if we are having a big roast for our main course, I would want a lighter style entrée, and some acid on the salad or the dessert (or both) to cut through the lamb fat that will be lingering on my palate.

Later in the book I outline a few balanced seasonal menus for three- or four-course family Sunday lunches or dinner parties, to offer some more examples for how to bring a few dishes together in harmony.

Read your cookbooks and explore; eat out and look around you. So many flavour combinations are right there waiting to be discovered and enjoyed.

Key Flavour Profiles

When we create and discuss dishes, we ultimately want a perfect balance – that's probably the most important part of a dish, aside from its seasonality. I've outlined below the eight main flavour profiles, if I can call them that – although technically a couple aren't flavours!

If you cook with an awareness of these key flavours and how you're combining them, then your dish will have a much better chance of being complete. That's not to say there's any guarantee: you can tick all the boxes, so to speak, but that won't necessarily mean perfection every time. I'll explain more about how to get these flavours working together on page 8.

1. Sweet

Sweetness can be found in many different forms aside from the obvious: sugar! Even though there are so many different types of sugar (brown, white, fine, caster, cane, demerara, granulated, icing and muscovado, to name a few) there are other ways to increase sweetness in a dish. You can use honey, maple syrup, corn syrup and molasses or even something like an aged balsamic vinegar. Natural sugars such as fructose found in fruit can also add a touch of sweetness to your dish without the need for additional ingredients. A surprising number of 'savoury' dishes have a sweet element.

2. Sour

When they think of sourness, most people instantly think of lemons, limes or grapefruit but the addition of something sour or acidic to a dish comes in multiple other forms. It could be something as simple as an acidic tomato, pickled vegetables, sour cream, yoghurt or even most fermented foods, such as kimchi or sauerkraut. Vinegars come in all different forms too: apple cider, balsamic, red or white wine, champagne, sherry. We always add a touch of acidity when we finish our sauces to really 'lift' the flavour profiles and cut through the fat content, ensuring a balanced palate.

3. Bitter

Don't underestimate this one, as bitterness is one of the five taste sensations that we are sensitive to, the others being salty, sour, sweet and savoury (these days commonly referred to as umami). We enjoy this flavour sensation probably more than we are aware: in coffee, chocolate, dark leafy greens, mustard, citrus peel and even beer! We would normally add something else to a bitter ingredient to offset its flavour profile, like sugar to coffee, cocoa and marmalades. Its bad rap probably comes from the fact that its main use for our ancestors was a way to help them identify toxic plants or foods.

4. Salty

One of my favourite flavour profiles. So much more than just sodium, saltiness can be introduced to a dish in many forms: soy, fish sauce, miso, even milk! There's the obvious table salt or sea salt too, of course, but the addition of anchovies, cheeses or cured meats and fish will also increase salt levels. But beware: while a perfectly seasoned dish is one of beauty, over season just a touch too much and it can end in disaster!

5. Spicy

This one is a little bit more of a personal flavour profile, depending on your preference for heat! But it's a lot more than red chillies, that's for sure. Spices such as cinnamon and different forms of pepper – black, white, pink or even fresh green peppercorns – all add an extra dimension. Ginger can have a wonderful natural heat, adding depth to a dish, and with crab I like just a splash of Tabasco or a pinch of cayenne to round off the palate, along with lime juice, salt and some fresh herbs.

6. Umami

The elusive 'fifth taste', until recently umami was kind of a secret that the Japanese kept to themselves! It refers to the 'savouriness' of a dish and relates to our detection of glutamate, an amino acid, in our food. Umami is found in natural forms in parmesan, mushrooms, tomatoes, meats, garum (a fish sauce from ancient Rome), seaweeds, miso, even Vegemite! Fermentation is another way of releasing the umami in foods, in items such as soy sauce, cheeses and cured meats.

7. Temperature

Whether it be fire, gas, coal, wood, ice, liquid nitrogen or even sous-vide cookery (cooking long and low in a sealed bag in a water bath), temperature plays a very important role in the fundamentals of all cooking. It can not only be used to cook a piece of meat or fish, for instance, and thereby change the chemical compounds and structure of the protein, but it can also bring an unexpected mouth sensation to any dish. That's what makes cold ice-cream with a hot pudding so satisfying!

8. Texture

The mouthfeel of a dish and contrasting textures can create a wonderful experience that elevates and excites the palate. And it's not all about crunch, either: creamy, sticky and even slimy textures all have a role to play in deciding what components you want to enjoy when finalising the elements of a complete meal. Think of how a sticky glaze elevates a roast duck, or how the soft, melting middle of a chocolate fondant makes it more exciting.

How to Marry Flavours

When thinking about what elements will be incorporated into a dish, I always try to use the key flavour profile as a guide, a 'roadmap' if you will, to ensure that what I'm cooking and creating is 'complete'. It's really all about the 'explosion' in the mouth, the way it feels: hot, cold, sweet, sour, crispy, crunchy, gooey, salty, savoury, bitter, spicy, soft . . . Bursts of flavour, temperature and texture, different sensations that excite. With an understanding of the ingredients and methods in this book, you'll learn to tinker with a dish as you make it to really fine-tune it, identify a missing ingredient that would complete it, or take a dish in an entirely different and unexpected direction for a new experience.

While I try to include many of the elements from my key flavour profile guide in each dish, it's not always applicable to each individual recipe. Of course, it also depends upon where the dish falls during the course of a meal, and the balance of the entire menu. I don't want to eat a lunch or a dinner that's full of salty and acidic items, but they have their place, and quite often finishing a meal with a sour or sweet dish can be complementary to what's come before.

So, time for my secrets to designing a dish.

Firstly, and I know it sounds simple, but what kind of meal do I want to eat? Do I want a big, long, lazy lunch, or am I after a more precise and refined dinner? This determines what and how I will cook, and what ingredients I'll search for.

A simple next step is to look around me. I take a moment to digest the seasons: what vegetables are at their peak? Is grass-fed beef at its prime? Have the first of the spring lambs started? Which herbs are plentiful and luscious? Are root vegetables in season, or are cherries, berries and figs bountiful? Start with the best possible produce and you give a dish every chance to shine.

One fact that's often overlooked is the weather. Is it a wonderful sunny, warm summer's day, or is it wet, miserable and stormy outside? It might sound strange (personally I don't think so) but my mood and my appetite are driven not only by the overall season, but more immediately by the day that's around me.

Once these questions are answered I can start to think about my core ingredients.

Is it a big protein, like roast pork or rib of beef with all the trimmings? Am I in the mood for the vegetables to be the star of the show or happy for them to be a support act? Do I feel like fish and seafood with a simple salad, something light and fresh?

Now the big decision: how do I cook what I want to eat? What will make it complete, balanced and, above all, delicious? That's where the key flavour profiles come in.

Take a simple tomato salad for instance. Do you think it's possible to tick all eight profiles? Let's try . . .

Okay, so we have some gorgeous ripe tomatoes. We cut them into various shapes and place them in a bowl. Tomatoes are naturally quite acidic, so that's a tick. To offset this, we can add a pinch of sugar and maybe a splash of aged balsamic vinegar: sweetness, tick.

Naturally you season the salad with sea salt and pepper, maybe even a splash of Tabasco, so those are ticks for salty and spicy. A little chopped chilli, perhaps. We can even bring in some more spice with the addition of herbs like rocket and basil, and maybe a fruity and peppery olive oil. For some bitterness we add bitter green leaves like radicchio or endive. Tick. Now the search for umami . . . It's found in lots of cheeses, so maybe some parmesan or an aged feta. These are umami, but also salty and textural. Tick, tick, tick! A few toasted croutons, warm from the pan, add some more texture and another temperature. Tick, tick.

So now you can see that what started off as a simple tomato salad develops depth of flavours and textures and a bit more complexity than just a few tomatoes in a bowl. But it's all about the balance: of the dressing, the bitter leaves and herbs, the amount of cheese and the hint of chilli or spice. It sounds simple, but the balance of a dish can sometimes be the hardest thing to get right. Too much salt: not good. Extremely bitter: quite unpleasant. Too many croutons: it becomes a sandwich!

Use this as a base guide for all dishes, break it down to its fundamental components and have fun exploring the endless possibilities.

Flavour Map

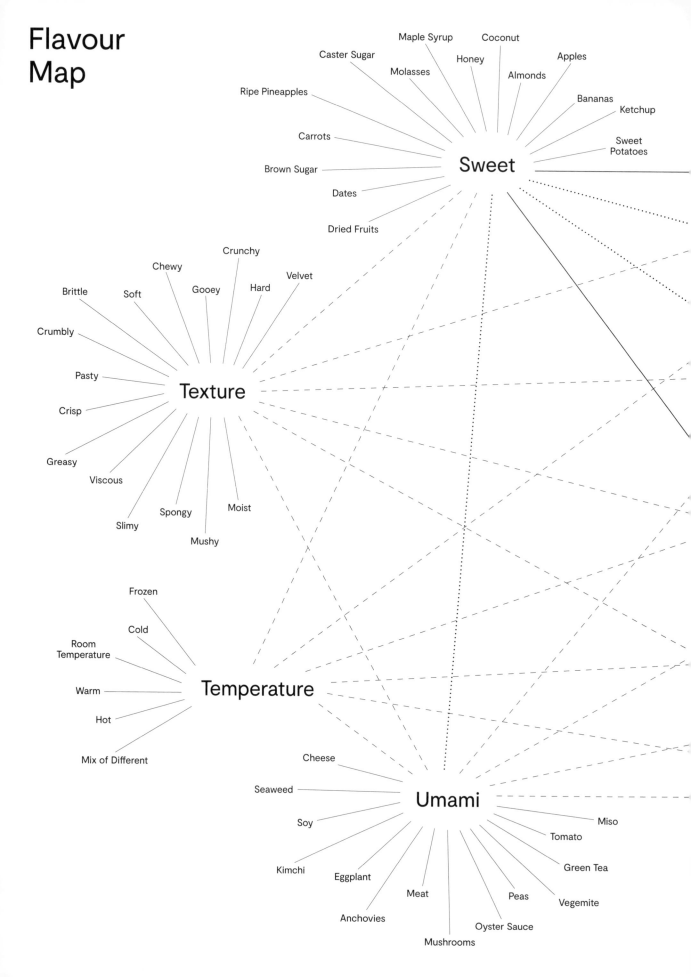

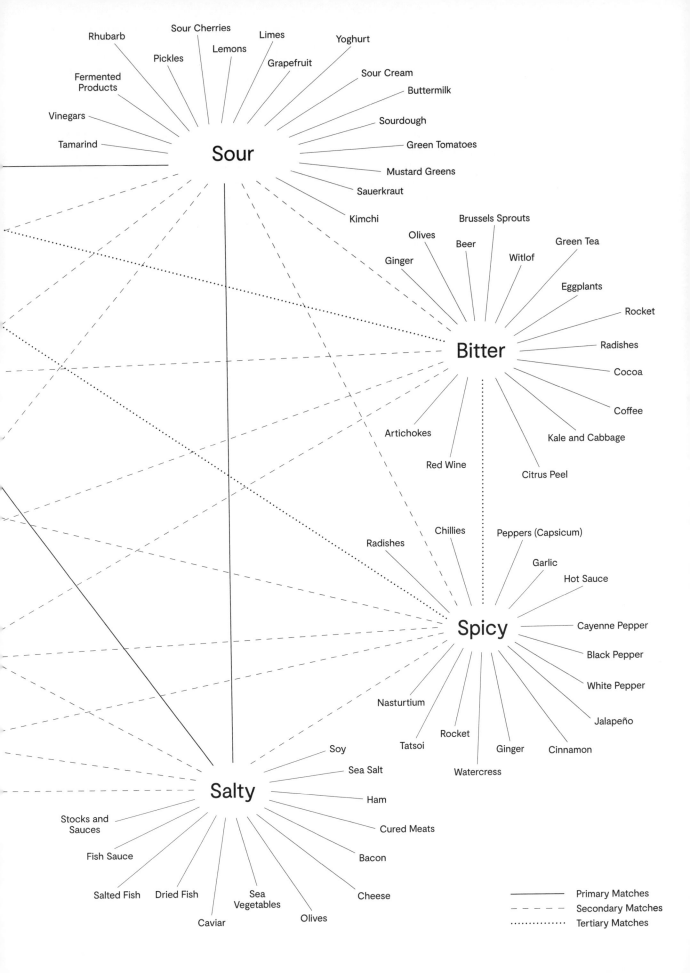

Sour

Tamarind
Vinegars
Fermented Products
Rhubarb
Pickles
Sour Cherries
Lemons
Limes
Grapefruit
Yoghurt
Sour Cream
Buttermilk
Sourdough
Green Tomatoes
Mustard Greens
Sauerkraut
Kimchi

Bitter

Ginger
Olives
Beer
Brussels Sprouts
Witlof
Green Tea
Eggplants
Rocket
Radishes
Cocoa
Coffee
Kale and Cabbage
Citrus Peel
Red Wine
Artichokes

Spicy

Chillies
Radishes
Peppers (Capsicum)
Garlic
Hot Sauce
Cayenne Pepper
Black Pepper
White Pepper
Jalapeño
Cinnamon
Ginger
Watercress
Rocket
Tatsoi
Nasturtium

Salty

Soy
Sea Salt
Ham
Cured Meats
Bacon
Cheese
Olives
Sea Vegetables
Caviar
Dried Fish
Salted Fish
Fish Sauce
Stocks and Sauces

———— Primary Matches
- - - - Secondary Matches
·········· Tertiary Matches

Using the Keys in this Book

In the top corner of each recipe you'll find the profile flavour keys and which ones out of the eight are the heroes in that particular dish. This will be a great reference point to help you understand what each recipe already has and you can build and evolve from there. The keys are what I hope will be a behind-the-scenes insight into the building blocks I've used to put together each recipe.

I've created these dishes to be complete and balanced already, and offer examples of how to synthesise flavours and textures that I know from experience work brilliantly together, but that's not to say they can't be adapted if you wish. There's room for flexibility and experimentation within the frameworks provided.

So, if a recipe featuring a sour profile asks for finger lime and you don't have any to hand, you can replace it with another sour ingredient such as lemon and be safe in the knowledge that you'll be keeping the dish in balance while trying something new. Or, if you're someone who loves bitter flavours, why not throw in an extra dash of verjus in the recipe for Rainbow Trout en Papillote, Fennel, Verjus (page 37) to up your enjoyment of the meal. Have fun playing around to suit your personal favourite flavours, and you'll soon learn what works best – and less well! (In terms of cooking times and temperatures, bear in mind that all of the recipes have been developed using a fan-forced rather than conventional oven. If using a conventional oven, you'll generally need to increase the temperature by 20°C, though cooking times may vary depending on your individual oven.)

Other helpful additions that I've added to each recipe are my market tips, chef's notes and drink pairings. (You'll notice there are no drink pairings for side dishes as these are served alongside mains, which already come with a corresponding drink recommendation. Two wines at the same time might be a bit much!) These provide more information on how I think: which wine would complement your meal, what to look for when you're out shopping or selecting your ingredients, why I use a certain technique . . . tips and tricks I've picked up over the years to make cooking a little easier.

It's one thing to be able to cook a dish from a technical perspective, but my aim here is to give you that little lightbulb moment around flavour to illuminate your cooking, so you can understand, develop and enjoy it even more.

A Guide to Seasonal Shopping

Supermarkets are a great convenience for us all these days, and the produce and selection are much better than when I was a kid, but to truly search for flavour you need to dig a little bit deeper. Farmers' markets offer a direct link to the grower and producer, and are a wonderful way to support small-scale farmers while getting the best seasonal produce available. They are popping up everywhere, and although they might be a little more expensive than other retail outlets, the quality is beyond compare.

Another place I really like to go to shop and enjoy the experience is an actual old-school market. In Melbourne the stand-out place for this is the Queen Victoria Market, but Preston Market is pretty cool too. What I love about these types of market is the characters: the personalities of the old Italian guy who's been selling tomatoes there for the past forty years; the Greek lady trying to get me to buy a second or third dip and take some of her olives too; the fishmonger who gives me a bigger fish than I really need, just because it's 'beauuudifuullll maaaate!'. Food really is all about people, after all.

Where I live, in Melbourne, we are also very lucky to have a huge multicultural community that influences what we cook and what we eat. The best thing about having people from all over the world is what they bring to the table, pardon the pun! Different ideas from different parts of the globe, all in one melting pot called Melbourne. These various cultures open the door to a whole new array of ingredients: so many different herbs and spices, unusual vegetables, oils, vinegars and sauces that make creating new dishes a total joy. And this is where shopping comes into play. Explore your nearby Asian grocery store for unfamiliar items, walk through the local Greek or Italian deli to pick up things you've never seen or tasted before. Ask questions of the shop owners, too – normally they are very happy to share secrets and part of their homeland with you.

One thing to remember when looking for produce, especially in Australia, is that because we are such a large country the seasons often blur into each other. As a result, produce that may be out of season in Melbourne, for instance, can simultaneously be at its peak in Queensland or Western Australia due to differences in climate and temperature. Take the humble strawberry for example. As someone born and bred in Melbourne, I always expect these to be around from late November or early December and run until February, sometimes even March, depending on the weather. But in Far North Queensland they are ripe and abundant around June or July, so thanks to interstate distribution they are readily available during the Melbourne winter – which just seems strange and foreign to me! Now, would I use them in the restaurant, serve a summer berry during a cold Victorian winter? No. Would I enjoy them at home with the kids, who love them (and probably aren't as concerned about seasonality as me)? Yes.

So, bear in mind that when I talk about seasonality, it's generally from a Melbourne point of view – not four seasons in one day, but certainly four seasons that are more distinct than in other parts of Australia. I'll let you decide what you want to eat, and when. Just remember: buying fruit, vegetables, fish and meat when they're in season and at their best is often the most cost-effective way to get the best product at the right price!

Produce by Season

Here are some of the most common fruit and vegetables and the times of the year when they're commonly in season. It's always worth bearing in mind that, as Australia is such a big country with many different climates, lots of things are actually available all year round nowadays. So, while this book provides a guide, be aware that some things are available outside of (or even opposite) the true season.

SPRING	SUMMER	AUTUMN	WINTER
Globe artichokes	Basil	Beans	Jerusalem artichokes
Asparagus	Beans	Beetroot	Broad beans
Beans	Beetroot	Brussels sprouts	Beetroot
Beetroot	Capsicums	Cabbages	Broccoli
Broad beans	Carrots	Capsicums	Brussels sprouts
Broccoli	Chillies	Carrots	Cabbages
Carrots	Corn	Cauliflower	Carrots
Cauliflower	Cucumbers	Celery	Cauliflower
Capsicums	Eggplants	Chillies	Celery
Chillies	Leeks	Corn	Leeks
Cucumbers	Lettuces	Cucumbers	Lettuces
Leeks	Onions	Eggplants	Onions
Lettuces	Parsley	Leeks	Parsley
Onions	Potatoes	Lettuces	Parsnips
Parsley	Rhubarb	Onions	Snowpeas
Parsnips	Silverbeet	Parsley	Potatoes
Peas (and snowpeas)	Spring onions	Parsnips	Rhubarb
Potatoes	Squash	Peas	Silverbeet
Rhubarb	Tomatoes	Potatoes	Spinach
Silverbeet	Zucchini	Rhubarb	Spring onions
Spinach		Silverbeet	Turnips
Spring onions		Spinach	
Squash	Bananas	Spring onions	Bananas
Zucchini	Blackberries	Squash	Grapefruit
	Blueberries	Sweet potatoes	Kiwifruit
	Cherries	Tomatoes	Lemons
Bananas	Grapes	Zucchini	Mandarins
Grapefruit	Melons		Oranges (navel)
Lemons	Nectarines		
Oranges (navel)	Oranges (valencia)	Apples	
	Peaches	Bananas	
	Plums	Figs	
	Raspberries	Grapes	
	Strawberries	Kiwifruit	
		Lemons	
		Watermelon	
		Nectarines	
		Peaches	
		Pears	
		Persimmons	
		Plums	
		Quinces	

Spring

I love spring.

Now don't get me wrong, I have a special place in my heart for each and every season, as individual and different as they might be, but there is something about the transition from the wet and windy, short, dark days and bitterly cold nights, to the joy of slightly warmer mornings and the knowledge that summer will soon be upon us.

I love the abundance of spring greens: the first asparagus spears and the assortment of peas and beans – snow, snap, butter, borlotti and broad. The way my garden just seems to come to life again almost overnight; the blossom on the trees and the flowers everywhere. Like most, I literally get a spring in my step – I'm excited by the thought of cooking with the new season's milk-fed baby lamb, perfect for lighter braises and slow-roasting. There's citrus, ready to be squeezed to add a burst of acid to sautéed spinach, creamed new leeks or a garlic dressing. Wait for that waft of aniseed when the fennel bulbs start appearing; the little hint of spice and pepper that the new season's radishes offer; the prickle on the globe artichokes, waiting to be prepared; a perfectly ripe avocado, ready to be smashed! And then there are all the leafy greens – cabbages, cavolo nero, silverbeet, spinach and chard – waiting to be eaten.

Sardine Escabeche

SERVES 4

1 teaspoon coriander seeds
1 teaspoon fennel seeds
2 star anise
300 ml extra virgin olive oil
2 baby carrots, finely sliced
2 golden shallots, peeled
    and finely sliced
1 celery stick, finely
    sliced diagonally
4 cloves garlic, finely sliced
50 ml red-wine vinegar
50 ml sherry vinegar
3 sprigs dill
2 bay leaves
3 sprigs thyme
pinch of saffron threads
1 teaspoon Spanish paprika or
    pimenton (smoked paprika)
finely grated zest and juice
    of 1 lemon
finely grated zest and juice
    of 1 orange
sea salt, to taste
24 fresh sardine fillets
½ fennel bulb, finely shaved

My interpretation of a classic Spanish dish that is also cooked in other parts of the Mediterranean, and certain parts of the Latin Americas. In its simplest form, this dish uses citrus or vinegars to cure and 'cook' the fish, and spices such as saffron or paprika for a little burst of flavour. Some variations simply cover the fish in the warm acidic liquid and cure it overnight, but in my version I like to fry the fish very quickly on the skin side first. This dish makes a great start to a meal, but I also like to use the leftovers for brekkie in my glamorous variation of sardines on toast.

Heat a saucepan over medium heat. Add the coriander seeds, fennel seeds and star anise and cook for a few minutes, shaking the pan occasionally, until lightly toasted. Remove from the pan and set aside to cool.

Heat 2 tablespoons of the olive oil in the pan and add the carrot, shallot, celery and garlic. Cook the vegetables over medium heat, stirring occasionally, until they are very soft but not coloured. Add both vinegars and cook until reduced by half.

Add the dill, bay leaves, thyme, saffron, paprika and the toasted coriander and fennel seeds. Stir in the zest and juice. Set aside 1 tablespoon of olive oil and stir the rest into the marinade. Heat without boiling, stirring until combined, and season with sea salt to taste. Set this marinade aside to cool to around 50°C (just warm).

Heat the remaining 1 tablespoon of olive oil in a heavy-based frying pan and sear the skin side of the sardine fillets. Transfer to a shallow glass or ceramic dish and pour the marinade over. Cover and refrigerate overnight.

To serve, remove the fish from the marinade and arrange on serving plates. Garnish with the shaved fennel and some of the vegetables and spices, and drizzle with some of the marinade.

CHEF'S NOTE

If you're not a sardine fan, this recipe also works well with red mullet, tuna, Spanish mackerel or any oily fish.

TO DRINK

A delicate and dry sherry from Andalucía in southern Spain. For this dish I would recommend a style commonly found in Sanlúcar de Barrameda, called Manzanilla. Because Sanlúcar is a coastal town, this delicate dry sherry develops a delicate salty/saline character as it ages and is a perfect accompaniment to acid-based fish dishes.

MARKET TIP

Always buy the best local olive oil you can afford. Try to taste whenever you can, as oils are a bit like wine and all very individual. I like to finish dishes with a little splash of peppery olive oil at the end for some extra 'pop'.

Scallops, Watercress, Sauce Agrume

SERVES 4

12 Port Phillip Bay (or similar)
    scallops in the half shell
extra virgin olive oil, to drizzle
1 bunch watercress,
    leaves picked
sea salt, to taste
freshly ground black pepper,
    to taste
1 tablespoon toasted
    pine nuts, to serve

SAUCE AGRUME
2 lemons
2 limes
2 oranges
2 grapefruit
100 ml extra virgin olive oil
100 ml grapeseed oil
2 tablespoons pine nuts, toasted
1 teaspoon coriander seeds,
    toasted and crushed
1 tablespoon sugar
1 sprig mint, leaves chopped
½ bunch chives, chopped
sea salt
freshly ground black pepper

Nothing quite beats eating a scallop from the shell. Or an oyster. Or a clam . . . and we're lucky to have a bounty of wonderful local Australian scallops. *Agrume* literally means 'citrus' in French, and using citrus at its peak is a perfect accompaniment to the briny and salty flavour of the scallop. There are a couple of methods for cooking the scallops: my preferences are either baked in the oven or just placed in the shell on the barbecue.

To make the sauce, finely grate the zest then juice one of each of the citrus fruit. Peel the remaining citrus fruit, cut the flesh into segments then chop. Combine the zest, juice and chopped flesh in a bowl. Add the oils, pine nuts, coriander seeds and sugar. Stir in the herbs just before serving and season to taste.

To prepare the scallops, remove from the shells and wash both the scallops and shells in lightly salted water. Discard all the outside membrane apart from the scallop itself, and the roe if desired. Place the scallop back into the washed shell.

Meanwhile, preheat a barbecue grillplate on high. Drizzle the scallops with a little olive oil, season with salt and pepper and place the shell directly onto the barbecue. After 3–4 minutes the scallops will start to sizzle. I like to eat my scallops just cooked, so this is enough cooking for me, but if you like your seafood cooked fully then leave the scallops on the barbecue a little longer.

To serve, arrange the scallops on a platter with the watercress and dress with the sauce agrume. Sprinkle with toasted pine nuts.

CHEF'S NOTE

This zingy citrus dressing is also great with other shellfish and crustaceans, and is a perfect match with grilled salmon fillets, too. Always add the chopped herbs just before serving so they remain bright green.

TO DRINK WITH THIS

I like using a fresh, neutral white wine with a hint of sweetness: the sweetness will highlight the sweetness of the scallops, while the neutrality will frame the flavours of the dish and carry it through to the finish. Use riesling from Mosel in Germany for an Old World wine and an off-dry riesling from South Australia for your New World fix.

MARKET TIP

Try to buy the best seafood you can find. We have an old saying in the kitchen: 'fresh is best'. Avoid frozen seafood where possible – it should look vibrant, bright and healthy.

Smoked Ham Hock and
Pea Soup, Mint Crème Fraîche

Umami . Texture . Sweet

SERVES 8–10

2 tablespoons olive oil
1 onion, sliced
1 leek, sliced
750 g fresh peas
2 sprigs mint
500 ml milk
500 ml cream
sea salt
freshly ground black pepper

HAM HOCK STOCK

3 good-quality smoked
    ham hocks
5 litres chicken stock or water
    (or enough to cover)
1 onion, halved
2 celery sticks
2 carrots, peeled and
    halved lengthways
½ bunch flat-leaf parsley
2 bay leaves
1 sprig thyme
1 sprig sage
10 black peppercorns
6 cloves
½ cinnamon stick

MINT CREME FRAICHE

200 ml crème fraîche
100 ml cream
½ bunch mint, leaves picked
    and finely chopped
sea salt
freshly ground black pepper

It's great being able to use one ingredient in different forms, such as the ham hock stock in this recipe for the soup, and the hock meat as a garnish – but any leftover smoked ham hock is also great to use in salads, terrines or even in a pie. What I love about this recipe is that the soup is a vibrant green colour with the smokiness of the hocks almost a hidden surprise in a delicious, velvety velouté.

To make the stock, combine the ham hocks and chicken stock or water in a large pot. Bring to a simmer over low heat and skim off any scum or impurities. Add the vegetables, herbs and spices and cook uncovered for about 4 hours, until the hocks are very tender.

Remove from the heat and allow the meat to cool in the stock. Once the meat and liquid have cooled, carefully remove the hocks from the stock and shred the meat into bite-sized pieces, discarding the skin and cartilage. Reserve the meat and pass the stock through a fine sieve to remove the solids.

Heat the oil in a large saucepan over medium heat. Gently cook the onion and leek, stirring occasionally, until soft but not coloured. Add the peas and mint.

Combine the milk, cream and 1 litre of the ham stock in another saucepan and bring to a rapid boil. Pour this hot liquid over the vegetables and cook until the peas are tender. The trick here is to cook the soup quickly, which preserves the colour of the peas.

Cool the soup rapidly to retain the beautiful 'spring' colour, then process in batches in a food processor until smooth. Season to taste with salt and pepper. Return to the pan and reheat to warm (50–60°C).

To make the mint crème fraîche, whisk the creams together until firm peaks form. Mix in the mint, and season to taste.

To serve, divide the soup between serving bowls, and add the ham hock meat. Garnish with a tablespoon of the mint crème fraîche.

CHEF'S NOTE

It's best to use fresh peas for this recipe if you can, but if you're time poor and still want to make your own soup, then frozen peas also do the job. And if you don't want a creamy soup, then use the ham hock broth with dried split peas and lots of vegetables like my nan used to. Nan used smoked bacon bones, too.

TO DRINK

I like using fruity wines to offset the smoky, salty flavour of the ham hock. Try a dry white from the sauvignon blanc grape. Look to more New World examples of this variety to pair with this dish. The inherent vegetal character of sauvignon blanc will pair perfectly with the peas.

MARKET TIP

Butchers are all a bit different and some specialise in certain things. At my restaurants we use lots of different butchers for different needs, and for smoked products it's best to find someone who specialises in smoking and curing. A good local German or Polish butcher will often have the best smoked pork products.

Cured Wagyu, Borlotti Beans, Sherry Vinegar

SERVES 6

150 g dried borlotti beans
2 pinches coarse salt
2 sprigs thyme
2 bay leaves
2 red capsicums, cut into
    large flat pieces
100 g broad beans, peeled
½ bunch chives, chopped
¼ bunch flat-leaf parsley,
    leaves picked and chopped
spring herbs such as wood
    sorrel, sheep's sorrel,
    nasturtium, snowpea shoots
    or marigolds, to serve
    (see Market Tip)

CURED WAGYU

100 g sea salt
100 g brown sugar
finely grated zest and juice
    of 2 limes
12 black peppercorns
6 juniper berries
1 sprig thyme
1 × 500 g piece wagyu rump

PICKLED SHALLOTS

100 ml water
50 ml white-wine vinegar
50 g sugar
2 golden shallots, sliced

DRESSING

1½ tablespoons sherry vinegar
1 teaspoon Dijon mustard
¼ cup extra virgin olive oil
pinch of sugar
sea salt
freshly ground black pepper

Curing things yourself is a wonderful process that takes time, patience, skill and love. As with any purchase, make sure you buy the best possible ingredients for curing that you can afford, and handle them with care. This recipe is just an overnight cure, so it needs to be started the day before, but if you want to make something like bresaola it takes a few weeks! It's a joy to use fresh borlotti beans when they are around – the season is short – but they can be substituted with dried ones if you can't find fresh, as I've done here. If you're not a big fan of wagyu, or find it a bit pricey, good grass-fed beef works well too.

Soak the dried borlotti beans overnight in cold water.

Meanwhile, to make the cured wagyu, process all the ingredients except the meat in a food processor until the peppercorns and berries are roughly ground and the ingredients are combined. Rub the mixture well into the meat. Place in a glass or ceramic dish, cover and refrigerate for 24 hours.

Next day, drain the water from the borlotti beans, place them in a large saucepan and cover with fresh cold water. Add the salt, thyme and bay leaves. Cook for 35–45 minutes or until just al dente. Drain well.

To make the pickled shallots, combine the water, vinegar and sugar in a medium saucepan and bring to the boil over medium heat. Remove from the heat and allow to cool slightly. Place the shallots in a bowl and pour over the warm brine. Bring to room temperature.

For the dressing, combine the vinegar and mustard in a bowl. Slowly add the olive oil, whisking to combine. Season with the sugar, sea salt and pepper to taste.

Cook the capsicum skin-side up under a hot grill until the skin is black and blistered. Set aside covered with foil to cool, then peel off the skin and cut the flesh into 2 cm squares. Combine with the borlotti beans, broad beans, pickled shallots, chives and parsley. Add the dressing and season to taste.

Just before serving, thinly slice the beef and arrange overlapping on serving plates, carpaccio-style. Spoon the bean mixture and dressing onto the beef and garnish with spring herbs.

CHEF'S NOTE

When curing or preserving always ensure that your work area, hands, containers etc are extremely clean. Curing is the 'cooking' process here and unlike other cooking techniques, there is no transfer of heat to kill any spores or bacteria.

TO DRINK

Using high quality dry madeira from Portugal is the pick here. Oxidised and aged fortified wines have a similar umami-rich flavour that's often present in cured meat so they're not only a match made in heaven but an interesting pairing that goes off the beaten track.

MARKET TIP

You could be a bit wild and use other types of legumes such as broad beans, snowpeas, butter beans or the good old green bean! If you have trouble finding 'exotic' herbs, then maybe try a local farmers' market.

Chicken Liver Parfait, Candied Cumquats, Brioche

Sweet . Umami . Texture

SERVES 10–12

CHICKEN LIVER PARFAIT
40 g butter
2 golden shallots, sliced
1 sprig thyme
6 black peppercorns
100 ml port
100 ml brandy
5 eggs
400 g soft butter
500 g chicken livers, cleaned
2 teaspoons sea salt
1 teaspoon freshly
 ground pepper

CANDIED CUMQUATS
300 g sugar
1 bay leaf
pinch of sea salt
300 ml water
250 g cumquats

1 × 500 g loaf brioche

Chicken parfait, or pâté as some Aussies like to call it, is a fantastic 'spread' (for lack of a better word) that keeps in the fridge for up to a week and is great to serve with charcuterie or even just on a lovely piece of toasted brioche. Sometimes I even like it on a piece of fresh white sliced! Its rich and luxurious texture makes it worth the effort of making it yourself, and it's actually a relatively cheap dish to make. Go on, treat yourself!

To make the parfait, preheat the oven to 120°C. Start first by making a reduction: melt the butter in a small saucepan over medium heat. Add the shallot, thyme and peppercorns and sweat down until soft, without colouring. Add the alcohol and cook until reduced by half. Pass the mixture through a fine sieve to remove solids, and allow to cool.

Combine the eggs and butter in a blender. Transfer to a jug. Blend the chicken livers until smooth. With the motor running, add the egg and butter mixture gradually, as if making mayonnaise. Once the mixture has emulsified, add the cooled reduction and the salt and pepper. Blend briefly to combine. If your blender is too small to purée the entire quantity at once, you may need to purée it in a couple of equal batches – but doing so will give you a better emulsion. Pass through a fine sieve.

Transfer the mixture to a 1 litre capacity ovenproof mould or terrine. Line a roasting pan with a folded clean tea towel, stand the mould on it and pour enough hot water into the pan to come halfway up the sides of the mould. Bake for 20–30 minutes, until the mixture is just wobbly. Remove from the oven and leave in the roasting pan to cool. When cool, remove the mould from the pan and place in the refrigerator overnight.

For the candied cumquats, combine the sugar, bay leaf, salt and water in a medium saucepan. Stir over medium heat to dissolve the sugar and salt. Bring to the boil, cool slightly and pass through a fine sieve.

Slice the cumquats and de-seed if required. Return the liquid to the saucepan and bring to the boil. Add the cumquats and cook over medium heat for 30–40 minutes, until tender. Set aside to cool in the liquid.

To serve, preheat the oven to 150°C. Thinly slice the brioche and warm it gently in the oven for 3–5 minutes. Slice some parfait and spread it onto the warm and crispy brioche, then serve with the candied cumquats. Some cornichons or pickled baby onions also make a nice addition.

CHEF'S NOTE

When making parfait, it is important to have all the ingredients at roughly the same temperature before beginning preparation. You are making a 'warm emulsion' – think hollandaise sauce – but here you are emulsifying the livers with eggs and butter, then cooking in a water bath to set the parfait.

TO DRINK

Parfait is a very intensely flavoured and rich dish that requires an equally intense wine to stand up to its flavour and texture. The age old classic pairing would be to use a sweet white wine from Sauternes in France or a botrytised dessert wine from Australia. Don't be afraid to use sweet wines before dry wines as this is something that is regularly practised in Europe.

MARKET TIP

As always, buy the freshest ingredients you can, but it's especially important with livers. Make sure they are bright red for chicken, or a deep burgundy for duck. Once cleaned, I like to soak them in milk overnight just to get rid of any strong 'gamey' flavour they may have.

Slow-cooked Chicken, Wild Garlic, Young Leeks

SERVES 4–6

1 × 1.6–1.8 kg free-range chicken
1 lemon, halved
1 bulb garlic, split into cloves
    (skins on)
2 bay leaves
2 sprigs thyme
2 sprigs rosemary
100 ml extra virgin olive oil
pinch of paprika
sea salt, to taste
freshly ground black pepper,
    to taste
2 golden shallots, peeled
2 bulbs new-season garlic,
    left whole
1 sprig marjoram
4 young leeks, trimmed
100 g bulbs wild garlic,
    including stalks and flowers,
    cloves peeled
1 preserved lemon, skin
    thinly sliced

Roast chicken is by far one of my favourite things to cook and eat. Simple, tasty and – so long as you use a really good-quality chicken – pretty easy. This dish is all about using garlic in a soft and subtle form, and different types of alliums (plants in the garlic and onion family). Wild garlic, young leeks, shallots and even black garlic can all be used to enhance the flavour of the chicken.

Preheat the oven to 170°C. To remove the chicken legs, place chicken on a chopping board and make small incisions in the skin on the thigh (this helps to keep the skin intact on the breast). Gently pull the leg down, and using a sharp knife cut round the 'oyster' and through the joint. Fill the cavity of the chicken with the lemon, garlic cloves, bay leaves and 1 sprig each of thyme and rosemary. Drizzle with half the olive oil and season with the paprika, salt and pepper.

Heat a large heavy-based pan over medium heat and sear the chicken crown gently until golden all over. Do the same with the legs, but on the skin side only. Place the crown on a rack in a roasting pan and add the legs, skin side up. Add the shallots and bulbs of new garlic along with the marjoram and remaining thyme and rosemary.

Roast the chicken, basting occasionally, and turn the shallots during cooking so they roast evenly. The legs and crown will probably cook at different times. Use a meat thermometer to test the crown, which will need to reach 65°C. Check after 30 minutes, then as needed up to 60–75 minutes in total. To ensure a succulent bird, set the chicken aside to rest for 20 minutes, loosely covered with foil. Place legs back in oven if needed making sure they are cooked properly – they should reach 72°C on the thermometer. Reserve the juice from the bottom of the cooking tray for serving.

Meanwhile, drop the leeks into a pot of boiling salted water and blanch for 2 minutes until tender. Refresh in a bowl of iced water. Drain and pat dry.

Heat the remaining olive oil in a saucepan over medium–low heat. Add the wild garlic cloves and stems and gently sweat until starting to wilt. Add the blanched leeks, preserved lemon skin, roasted shallots and roasted garlic cloves. Season well and finish with the garlic flowers.

Reheat the chicken in a hot oven for 6–8 minutes before taking the breasts off the bone, and portion as required.

On a large serving platter, arrange the wild garlic and leek mixture then lie the chicken legs and the breasts on top. To finish, drizzle the cooking juice over the chicken.

CHEF'S NOTE

This recipe is a bit different as I 'joint' the chicken before cooking, as opposed to roasting it whole. It's a bit easier to handle and marinate, and saves you carving the cooked bird later too. I've separated the breast (and crown) from the legs here as they take different amounts of time to cook.

TO DRINK

The classic pairing of chardonnay and chicken is still one of my favourites. I like to look at wines from the Yarra Valley or Margaret River here. The trick is to not use overtly oaky or buttery styles, but rather wines that have a balance of ripe fruit and oak. Try Voyager Estate chardonnay from WA or Wantirna Estate chardonnay from the Yarra.

MARKET TIP

You'll need to do a little foraging for the wild garlic, but it's easy to find – look alongside footpaths, in woodland or hedgerows, and riverbanks.

Coral Trout, Coriander, Ginger, Sweet-and-sour Salad

SERVES 4-6

1 × 1.5–2 kg coral trout,
    scaled and cleaned
sea salt

MARINADE

1 tablespoon coriander seeds
1 tablespoon fennel seeds
3 star anise
3 cm piece ginger, peeled
    and roughly chopped
1 lemongrass stalk,
    roughly chopped
4 garlic cloves
2 green chillies, seeded
    and roughly chopped
2 golden shallots,
    roughly chopped
finely grated zest and juice
    of 2 limes
½ bunch coriander,
    roughly chopped

FRIED SHALLOTS

2 banana shallots
vegetable oil
sea salt

DRESSING

1½ tablespoons palm sugar
2 tablespoons sugar
finely grated zest and juice
    of 2 limes
100 ml fish sauce
3 cloves garlic, sliced
1 long green chilli, finely chopped
1 long red chilli, finely chopped
3 cm piece ginger, finely grated
100 ml peanut oil

SALAD

½ Lebanese cucumber
1 carrot
1 small daikon or white radish
3 spring onions
1 bunch Thai basil, leaves picked
½ bunch mint, leaves picked
1 bunch coriander, leaves picked
1 red chilli, sliced
200 g beansprouts

There are so many different ways to enjoy eating fish and seafood, but nothing beats a whole baked fish. It stays moist and juicy, looks fantastic in the centre of the table and is a great meal to share with family and friends. Coral trout is a highly regarded eating fish, with a wonderful texture and an amazing sweet taste. Being from warmer waters and a tropical climate, it marries perfectly with ginger, and a refreshing sweet-and-sour salad.

For the marinade, heat a saucepan over medium heat. Add the coriander seeds, fennel seeds and star anise and cook for a few minutes, shaking the pan occasionally, until lightly toasted. Remove from pan and set aside to cool. Blend all the marinade ingredients in a food processor. Season with salt to taste. Gently rub into the fish, inside and out. Cover and leave in the fridge to infuse for at least 30 minutes or, for a really great result, overnight.

Preheat the oven to 210°C. Line a rimmed baking tray with foil and place the fish on it. Bake for about 45–50 minutes, until the flesh flakes when tested with the point of a small knife. Leave to rest for 15 minutes.

Meanwhile, to make the fried shallots, finely slice or julienne the shallots. Place in a pan and cover with cold vegetable oil. Deep-fry on medium heat for 30 minutes until golden brown. Remove shallots from oil with a slotted spoon and place on kitchen paper to absorb excess oil, then season with salt.

To make the dressing, mix the sugars, zest, juice and fish sauce to make a soft paste. Add the garlic, chilli, ginger and peanut oil. Taste to ensure it has a good balance of sweet, hot and sour – and adjust accordingly!

For the salad, I like to have different textures, shapes and sizes all working together so this is a chance to 'freestyle'! My suggestion would be to shave the cucumber lengthways on a mandolin, finely julienne the carrot, slice thin discs of daikon or white radish, and slice the spring onions diagonally – but it's completely up to you! Add the Thai basil, mint and coriander leaves, sliced chilli and beansprouts and combine.

To serve, place the baked fish on a large serving platter. Dress the salad with enough of the dressing to taste and the fried shallots, and serve with the fish.

CHEF'S NOTE

Make sure that when cooking fish whole, you check that all the 'insides' have been removed and look for any random scales left on by the fishmonger. I always give whole fish a quick once over before preparing them and take off any large spikey fins with scissors.

TO DRINK

A delicate dry white wine is the best option here. Try using the intensely citric rieslings from the Clare Valley or a young fresh semillon from the Hunter Valley. These wines are almost always in the lemon/lime spectrum and when using them, think of it as taking a big wedge of lemon or lime and squeezing it across the fish.

MARKET TIP

If you can't find coral trout, then don't be afraid to substitute another firm white flesh fish, like snapper or barramundi. The sweet-and-sour salad also goes very well with shellfish, especially crayfish!

Roasted Leg of Lamb, Rainbow Chard, Sauce Paloise

SERVES 4–6

LAMB

1 × 2–2.5 kg leg milk-fed lamb
sea salt
freshly ground black pepper
150 ml extra virgin olive oil
finely grated zest of 1 lemon
½ bunch rosemary,
   leaves chopped
½ bunch thyme,
   leaves chopped
2 tablespoons Dijon mustard
10 cloves garlic, finely chopped

RAINBOW CHARD

2 bunches rainbow chard,
   washed thoroughly
100 ml extra virgin olive oil
50 g butter or lamb dripping
3 cloves garlic, finely sliced
finely grated zest and juice
   of 1 lemon
pinch of freshly grated nutmeg

SAUCE PALOISE

6 egg yolks
50 ml tarragon vinegar
50 ml warm water
juice of ½ lemon
250 g butter, melted and
   still warm
1 bunch mint, leaves picked
   and finely chopped
sea salt
freshly ground black pepper

When I think of spring, my first thought is lovely new-season lamb. We like to use Flinders Island milk-fed lamb: the flavour and quality are unsurpassed. This dish also takes me back to my childhood when my mum and my grandmother, Audrey, used to cook us a Sunday roast dinner as a family treat, with all the trimmings, and if we were lucky, dessert too! Sauce paloise is one of those great derivatives of hollandaise, a classic egg emulsion sauce rich with butter and spiked with mint.

For the lamb, preheat the oven to 160°C. Use kitchen string to tie the leg up tight so it holds its shape and is firm to the touch. Season well with salt and pepper. Heat a large pan over medium–high heat and sear the lamb until it is golden all over. Place the lamb on a rack in a roasting pan. Combine the olive oil, lemon zest, rosemary, thyme, mustard and garlic. Brush all over the lamb, keeping some to use later.

To cook the meat to blushing pink, roast for 1 hour, occasionally brushing with the reserved oil mixture. Test with a meat thermometer inserted into the thickest part of the meat, but not touching the bone. The temperature should be about 55°C. Allow to rest for 20 minutes.

To prepare the chard, separate the leaves from the stems. Keep the leaves whole and trim the ends of the stems on the diagonal. Heat the oil and butter in a large heavy-based pan over medium heat until the butter foams gently. Add the garlic and cook until golden and fragrant. Add the chard stems first and cook for 1 minute, then add the leaves and let them wilt down, adding a splash of water if needed to create steam, for a few minutes or until nearly tender. Add the zest and juice, grate some nutmeg over, and season to taste. The stems should be tender and the chard green with a delicious citrus flavour.

To make the sauce, put a pan of water on to simmer. In a heatproof bowl that will sit comfortably over the pan, combine the egg yolks, tarragon vinegar, warm water and half of the lemon juice. Place the bowl over the pan (make sure the base of the bowl doesn't touch the water) and whisk until the mixture is thick and forms a ribbon when drizzled back over itself. Remove from the heat. Slowly add the butter in a steady stream, whisking constantly until incorporated. If it looks too thick, add a touch of warm water. Mix in the mint and the remaining lemon juice, and season well with salt and pepper.

Serve the sliced lamb drizzled with sauce paloise, with chard on the side.

CHEF'S NOTE

When cooking larger cuts of meat, if possible it's always better to cook the meat on the bone. It stays juicier and doesn't shrink as much and also seems to have a better flavour. Try it and you'll see the difference.

TO DRINK

This is an incredibly versatile dish that can be paired with a number of different wines. The most important thing to consider here is savouriness. Steer away from wines that have a sweeter fruit profile. Try cabernet sauvignon-based wines from the Medoc in Bordeaux or mourvèdre-based wines from areas like Bandol in the south-west of France.

MARKET TIP

It's always better and cheaper to buy produce when it's in season and at its peak, and lamb is no exception. Ask your butcher for the best new-season lamb they have, ensuring it's a nice pale pink for milk-fed, or a rosy red for grass-fed lamb. If you want to truss or tie your lamb, ask for some butcher's (kitchen) string too. Choose chard that is vibrant, crisp and fresh.

Roast Duck, Turnips, Blood Orange

Sweet . Spicy . Umami

SERVES 4–6

SAUCE
8 duck wings or necks, chopped
2 golden shallots, sliced
1 carrot, finely chopped
1 celery stick, finely chopped
2 cm piece ginger, sliced
100 ml red-wine vinegar
200 ml blood orange juice
1 litre duck or chicken stock

GLAZE
150 ml honey
150 ml blood orange juice
1 teaspoon soy sauce
finely grated zest of
    2 blood oranges

DUCK
1 × 2–2.2 kg duck
2 blood oranges, cut
    into wedges
2 cm piece ginger, sliced
1 sprig thyme
1 lemongrass stalk, chopped
½ bunch coriander,
    roughly chopped
sea salt
freshly ground black pepper

TURNIPS
50 ml grapeseed oil
2 bunches baby turnips,
    trimmed and peeled
50 g butter
honey (optional)
50 ml duck or chicken stock

Roast duck always seems like a special occasion kinda dish for me, but it shouldn't be . . . it's just like an extra tasty chicken! Duck and orange is a classic combination, but using blood oranges adds extra depth of flavour and a slight bitterness that adds complexity to the sauce. I use a classic French technique here with a touch of Asia from the ginger and honey, while the turnips make a perfect accompaniment.

To make the sauce, preheat the oven to 180°C. Place the wings or necks in a heavy flameproof roasting pan. Roast for 10 minutes or until golden brown. Add the shallot, carrot, celery and ginger to the pan and roast for a few minutes, until golden. Strain all the fat out. Add the vinegar, place over medium heat on the stovetop and cook until reduced to a glaze. Add half the juice and cook until reduced by half, then repeat with the remaining juice. Add the stock and cook for 45–60 minutes until reduced by half. Pass through a fine sieve into a clean saucepan. Simmer over medium heat and reduce to your desired consistency.

For the glaze, combine the honey, juice and soy sauce in a saucepan and simmer over a medium heat until sticky like honey. Add the zest and set aside to cool.

For the duck, preheat the oven to 180°C. Fill the cavity with the orange wedges, ginger, thyme, lemongrass and coriander. Use kitchen string to truss the bird, making sure the legs are tied nice and tight. Season with salt and pepper. Heat a large heavy-based frying pan over medium heat and sear the duck all over until beautifully golden and caramelised.

Place the duck on a rack in a roasting pan and bake for around 45 minutes, brushing occasionally with the glaze so it becomes sticky, sweet and delicious. The legs and breast will cook at different times, so test them with a meat thermometer every 20 minutes. You want the crown to be pink and cooked to around 55°C so remove from the oven at 45°C and after a rest the breasts should have risen perfectly to 55°C. Remove the legs from the duck, and if needed (they should reach 72°C) place back in the oven, skin side up, to finish cooking. Rest the duck for 15–20 minutes.

Heat the grapeseed oil in a frying pan over medium heat and add the baby turnips. Cook gently, turning to make sure they cook evenly, until tender. Add 30 g of the butter and toss to coat, and you can add a spoonful of honey to help caramelise the turnips if you like. When they are almost tender, strain away the fat and add the duck stock and remaining butter. Gently turn the turnips through the glaze.

Pop the duck back in the oven for 6–8 minutes to warm before taking off the bone. Warm the sauce in a saucepan. Just before serving, brush the meat with the glaze again so it's sticky and delicious. Serve with the turnips and sauce.

CHEF'S NOTE

Some people like their duck fully cooked, but I like to have my duck breasts cooked to a lovely medium. However, when roasting the duck whole, the breasts are ready well before the legs! To fix this problem, I cook the duck whole and when the breast is ready I remove the legs and finishing cooking them separately. This way I have the best of both worlds!

TO DRINK

Duck and pinot noir is a match made in heaven, but I think nebbiolo and duck should be spoken of in the same breath. The nebbiolos produced in Piedmonte, Italy are the purest expression of this variety – the best examples offer up flavours of dried berries, burnt citrus, game meat, earth and mushrooms. The tannins in nebbiolo are firm, which helps to cut through the fattiness of duck.

MARKET TIP

Don't use standard large turnips for this recipe. Baby turnips are a nicer alternative because they are a little bit sweeter plus they look lovely too. They're around in early spring.

Rainbow Trout en Papillote, Fennel, Verjus

SERVES 4

4 × 400–500 g baby rainbow
    trout, scaled and cleaned
2 lemons, sliced
2 fennel bulbs, sliced
4 cloves garlic, sliced
1 bunch dill
50 ml extra virgin olive oil
sea salt
white pepper
1 tablespoon fennel seeds
50 ml verjus

Don't be scared by the fancy term 'en papillote': it's just
a French word that's used to describe the cooking method.
The food is placed inside a bag made of baking paper before
being baked in the oven, or sometimes I even like to do it
outside on the barbecue. This technique steams the fish and
keeps it nice and moist while cooking, plus the bag seals in the
flavours from the herbs and spices, making it super tasty!

Preheat the oven to 180°C.

Open up each trout and put lemon, fennel, garlic and dill inside the
cavities. Drizzle with olive oil and season with salt, white pepper and
fennel seeds, then fold the cavities closed again.

Place fish onto sheets of baking paper. Add verjus. To seal, join the
top and bottom edges of the baking paper, fold them over themselves
a few times, then twist the two ends and tie with kitchen string in order
to close them.

Place bags onto an oven tray and bake for 12 minutes. Once cooked,
remove from the oven and serve the trout on individual plates in their
paper bags, to be opened at the table. A fresh and crispy salad would
make the perfect accompaniment.

CHEF'S NOTE

Make sure that you seal the bag nice and
tight – you want the steam to be captured
inside the parcel so the fish cooks evenly
and the flavours are trapped. You don't
have to use whole fish for the recipe
either; it works just as well for single
portions too.

TO DRINK

I recently came across a grape variety
called assyrtiko that is commonly grown
on the Greek island of Santorini. This
fresh dry white is almost riesling-like in
its approach but shows a distinct salty/
saline character that really brings out
the flavour of seafood. For a New World
alternative, Jim Barry of the Clare Valley
has just released the first example of this
variety in Australia.

MARKET TIP

If you can't find rainbow trout or are
not a big fan of freshwater fish, this dish
works really well with other fish too: think
salmon, whiting, garfish or even flathead.

Spring Salad

SERVES 4–6

extra virgin olive oil,
   for greasing and drizzling
1 kohlrabi, quartered
2 red onions, quartered
8 baby carrots
2 young leeks
10 yellow beans, trimmed
10 green beans, trimmed
12 asparagus spears, trimmed
10 snowpeas, trimmed
1 avocado, peeled and quartered
8 small radishes, halved
1 fennel bulb, finely shaved
1 witlof, broken into
   individual leaves
250 g green leaves of your
   choice, such as baby
   spinach, endive or tatsoi
fresh herbs to finish, such
   as parsley, chervil, chives
   or tarragon

DRESSING
100 ml extra virgin olive oil
50 ml hazelnut oil
50 ml red-wine vinegar
1 tablespoon Dijon mustard
pinch of salt
pinch of sugar

There is no better side dish or salad that captures the true essence of spring as well as this one. The ingredients can vary depending upon what you find at the markets, so feel free to use a little creative licence when it comes to selecting your spring vegetables for this.

Preheat the oven to 180°C. Oil a large baking tray and arrange the kohlrabi, onion, carrots and leeks on it. Drizzle generously with olive oil and roast for 10 minutes, at which point remove the carrots. Return the other vegetables to the oven for a further 10 minutes, until tender and caramelised.

Bring a large saucepan of water to the boil and prepare a large bowl of iced water. Drop the beans into the saucepan and cook for 2 minutes. Lift out with tongs or a slotted spoon and drop into the iced water to cool quickly. Drain and pat dry with paper towel. Repeat with the asparagus, cooking for 1 minute, and the snowpeas for 30 seconds.

To make the dressing, combine all the ingredients in a bowl and whisk until emulsified.

Arrange the roasted, blanched and fresh vegetables and leaves and herbs on a serving platter and drizzle with dressing just before serving.

CHEF'S NOTE

Whenever I construct a dish I always think about the balance. So, for a composed salad like this, think about texture, sweet, sour, and raw with cooked. The best example of this is Michel Bras in Laguiole, France and his signature dish, gargouillou. It's a dish that changes and evolves throughout the season, but more importantly the months, weeks and even days, depending on what is best and available.

MARKET TIP

Get creative and experiment with different produce. Try lovely sweet fresh peas raw from the pod, fried kale for a bit of crunch, pickled shallots for some acid, and nuts or pulses. Basically, I just buy whatever looks fresh and vibrant that I think would make this salad delicious – and make sure you use plenty of fresh herbs, too!

New Season's Asparagus, Broken Egg, Black Truffle

SERVES 6

4 bunches green asparagus
4 eggs
50 ml verjus
50 ml champagne vinegar
1½ teaspoons Dijon mustard
200 ml extra virgin olive oil,
      plus extra to drizzle
¼ bunch chives, finely chopped
¼ bunch chervil, leaves
      finely chopped
¼ bunch flat-leaf parsley,
      leaves finely chopped
2 tablespoons tarragon leaves,
      finely chopped
1 large golden shallot,
      very finely chopped
sea salt
freshly ground black pepper
pinch of sugar
½ lemon
25 g black truffle, finely chopped

Of all the spring ingredients that come to life when the warmer months arrive, asparagus must be close to my favourite. Okay, it is! A versatile vegetable that is just as tasty hot, cold, raw or cooked. While its aphrodisiac powers are not proven scientifically, it never hurts to eat plenty of the *points d'amour* when in season! The prestige of black truffle in this dressing really does take this dish to the next level, and if you can afford them, make sure you use them!

Bring a large saucepan of salted water to the boil. Prepare a large mixing bowl filled with iced water to cool the asparagus after cooking. Wash the asparagus under cold water and remove the woody ends.

Divide the asparagus into two batches. Drop the first batch into the boiling water. Cook for 2 minutes if the asparagus is large, and 90 seconds if small. Transfer the asparagus from the boiling water to the iced water, and then repeat this process with remaining asparagus. Once the asparagus is thoroughly chilled, drain well and set aside until required.

Submerge the eggs in cold water in a saucepan, and place over medium–high heat. Prepare another bowl of iced water. As soon as the water reaches the boil, remove the pan from the heat and leave the eggs to sit for 3 minutes. Transfer the eggs to the iced water and leave to cool.

Peel 2 of the eggs and place in a food processor with the verjus, vinegar and mustard. With the motor running, slowly pour in the oil to create a thick emulsion. Transfer to a bowl and fold in the herbs and shallot. Season with salt, pepper and sugar. Peel the remaining eggs and break them into the dressing. Mash with a fork to form a chunky, herbaceous sauce.

To serve, place the asparagus on a serving platter and drizzle with a little olive oil. Season with salt, pepper and a squeeze of lemon juice. Drizzle the sauce over the asparagus in thick lines, and sprinkle with truffle.

CHEF'S NOTE

If blanching asparagus, always use a large amount of heavily salted water, boiling rapidly. Normally 2 teaspoons salt per litre is about right. Cook for less than 2 minutes and plunge into iced water so the asparagus stays a vibrant green and remains nice and crunchy.

MARKET TIP

Make sure you source the best eggs you can find for this dressing. Super fresh, real free range and organic eggs make it so much more than the sum of its parts. And don't be afraid to use different eggs, too – duck eggs are wonderful, and if you can be bothered peeling them, soft boiled quail eggs add a touch of class to any dish.

Duck Fat Roasted Potatoes, Herb Salt

SERVES 4–6

1 kg roasting potatoes
20 g sea salt
1 tablespoon black
    peppercorns
5 sprigs thyme
1 sprig rosemary
1 bay leaf
5 cloves garlic, unpeeled
200 g duck fat
50 ml olive oil
1 tablespoon thyme
    leaves, picked
1 tablespoon rosemary

HERB SALT

1 tablespoon rosemary, chopped
1 teaspoon dried thyme
1 teaspoon dried oregano
1 teaspoon dried basil
1 teaspoon freshly ground
    black pepper
250 g salt

Is there anything tastier than an old school roast potato? My grandmother, Audrey, used to make the best ones I've ever tasted, and while I think mine are pretty special, they still don't match hers. I think the missing ingredient must be love: there is nothing better than a Sunday roast cooked by someone special in your life. That's not to say I don't cook mine with plenty of love, passion and a pretty solid technique, it just seems to taste better when you're a child and your nan cooks them for you!

To make the herb salt, mix all ingredients in a bowl.

Peel the potatoes and cut into large evenly-sized pieces, so they cook at the same time. Place into a large saucepan with the salt, pepper, herb sprigs, bay leaf and garlic. Cover with plenty of water, place over medium heat and bring to a simmer. Cook the potatoes until they are tender. Be careful – they must be tender, but not falling apart. Gently drain the potatoes and spread out in a single layer on a tray. Leave in the fridge overnight, uncovered, in order to allow a slight skin to form on the outside.

Preheat the oven to 210°C. Place a large roasting pan in the oven to heat. In a small saucepan, melt the duck fat with the olive oil until hot and combined.

When the roasting pan is very hot, add the oil mixture and then the potatoes. Toss the potatoes in the oil and return the pan to the oven for 15–20 minutes, or until the potatoes begin to form a lovely golden brown crust. Add the thyme leaves and rosemary, and stir the potatoes to expose the uncooked sides. Return to the oven and finish cooking for a further 10–15 minutes. Once the potatoes are a nice, crispy brown, season with herb salt and serve.

Note: This makes more herb salt than you will need for this recipe. It can be used to season just about anything. Store in an airtight container in a cool dark place for up to 4 weeks.

CHEF'S NOTE

Such a simple dish like this is all about planning. Buy the perfect roasting spud, and once par-boiled I like to dry mine out uncovered in the fridge overnight. This removes the excess moisture from the potato to give it a nice crusty outside when roasted.

MARKET TIP

The sugar and starch content of potatoes changes throughout the year, so make sure you buy the right potato at the right time. Sounds simple, but it's not! I find that less common varieties like royal blue, king edward or kennebec are best in spring, but a waxy variety like desiree, sebago or golden delight work well too.

Globe Artichokes, Saffron, Shallots

SERVES 4-6

¼ cup grapeseed oil
2 brown onions, chopped
1 fennel bulb, chopped
5 cloves garlic, chopped
750 ml chardonnay,
    or other crisp white wine
1 orange
4 lemons
1 tablespoon black peppercorns
1 tablespoon coriander seeds
2 sprigs thyme
1 litre chicken stock
good pinch of saffron
16 large globe artichokes
16 golden shallots, peeled
6 baby carrots (about 150 g)
60 g butter, chopped
½ bunch flat-leaf parsley,
    leaves chopped
sea salt
freshly ground black pepper

While they can be a bit time consuming to prepare, fresh artichokes are definitely worth the effort. They're great roasted, steamed or cooked in the classic French technique, *barigoule*, and are a great accompaniment for grilled fish, lamb and beef.

Heat the oil in a large wide saucepan over medium heat. Add the onion, fennel and garlic and cook, stirring occasionally, until translucent. Add the wine and bring to the boil.

Cut the orange and one of the lemons in half. Add to the pan, along with the peppercorns, coriander seeds, thyme and the chicken stock. Simmer for 10 minutes, then add the saffron.

Fill a large mixing bowl with iced water and add the juice from remaining three lemons. Working one at a time, cut the stem of an artichoke about 2 cm below the flower, then cut about 5 cm from the top of the artichoke, so the top is flat. Peel back and remove the tough outer green leaves until you get to the golden yellow layer.

Using a paring knife, move in a circle around the outside of the artichoke to clean away the remaining smaller green leaves, then peel the base and stem of the artichoke so that no green remains – only the succulent yellow interior. Use a melon baller or teaspoon to scoop out the fuzzy purple choke from the centre. Work quickly, then submerge the whole artichoke, flower-side down, in the acidulated iced water. The faster you peel and soak the artichokes, the more vibrantly coloured they will be in the end.

Scoop the trimmed artichokes from the acidulated water with a slotted spoon and transfer to the wine and stock mixture. Cover the surface with a round of baking paper to keep the artichokes submerged. Bring to the boil, then reduce to a simmer and cook for 10 minutes. Add the shallots and cook for another 15–20 minutes, or until the stems of the artichokes are very tender and the shallots can be easily pierced with a knife. Remove from the heat and set aside to cool.

Slice the baby carrots on an angle, 5 mm thick. Blanch for 2 minutes in a pan of salted boiling water.

To serve, remove the shallots and artichokes from the liquid, reserving the liquid. Bring the liquid to the boil over medium–high heat and cook until reduced to a thick syrup. Cut the artichokes in half at this point if they are very large. Return the artichokes, shallots and carrot to reheat and glaze in the saffron syrup. Add the butter and the parsley and stir until emulsified. Season with salt and pepper.

CHEF'S NOTE

When peeling artichokes, it's always good to wear gloves. This prevents your hands from staining and helps save you from the prickles!

MARKET TIP

When choosing globe artichokes, try and pick the firmest and most 'closed' artichokes you can find. Although they last a while after being harvested, they can quite quickly become limp, and the flower itself starts to open up.

Charred Corn, Green Chilli, Lime

SERVES 4

6 long green chillies
2 tablespoons grapeseed oil,
    plus extra for the corn
1 golden shallot, chopped
3 cloves garlic, chopped
1 teaspoon cayenne pepper
250 g unsalted butter, at room
    temperature, chopped
½ bunch coriander, leaves
    picked and chopped
½ bunch flat-leaf parsley,
    leaves picked and chopped
sea salt
juice of 2 limes
8 corn cobs
smoked paprika, to season
lime wedges, to serve

Whole grilled, charred or simply boiled, corn is one of my favourite things to eat. Grabbing the cob in my hands, eating the sweet delicious sweet kernels while hot and buttery, is one of life's simplest yet most rewarding pleasures. This recipe adds a touch of green chilli for some extra zing, and a bit of lime for that citrus burst. Sprinkle with sea salt and spread on the chilli butter: superb!

Preheat a barbecue grillplate over high heat. Toss 4 of the chillies in a little grapeseed oil to coat. Cook until blackened, then place in a bowl and cover with plastic wrap. Leave to steam and cool. Heat the remaining oil in a small saucepan over medium heat and cook the shallot and garlic until soft but not coloured. Set aside to cool.

Slip the blackened skins from the chillies and remove the seeds. Dice the flesh finely and place in a food processor with the shallot and garlic mixture and the cayenne pepper, butter, coriander and parsley. Process until well combined, then add the lime juice and process again.

Transfer the butter to a bowl. Remove the seeds from the remaining raw chillies and finely dice the flesh. Fold through the butter, then season with salt. Set aside at room temperature.

Peel back the husk of the corn, rub the kernels with grapeseed oil and season with salt. Cook on the grillplate over high heat for 8–10 minutes, rotating occasionally to cook all sides, until vibrant yellow with deep black grill marks.

To serve, drench the corn in the chilli butter (you cannot put too much!) and season with salt and paprika. Serve with lime wedges to squeeze over.

CHEF'S NOTE

When cooking corn in salted water I always like to leave the husk on – it protects the kernels from rapid and vigorous boiling, and adds flavour to the water when cooking, almost like making a corn stock.

MARKET TIP

This dish is great with large corn cobs, but when the baby sweetcorn season is in full swing, treat yourself and buy the little whole gems. You should be able to find these at most farmers' markets these days or ask your local fruit and veg guy to put some aside for you.

Roasted Rhubarb,
Burnt Vanilla Custard

SERVES 6–8

1 kg rhubarb
100 g caster sugar
finely grated zest of 2 limes
    or lemons
finely grated orange zest,
    to serve

BURNT VANILLA CUSTARD
550 ml cream
200 ml milk
1 vanilla bean, split,
    seeds scraped
150 g egg yolks (about 7)
100 g caster sugar

OAT BISCUIT (OPTIONAL)
200 g oats
50 g plain flour
100 g caster sugar
2 tablespoons honey

Rhubarb and custard! What an absolute classic, memory-filled combination. I'm sure everyone has their own interpretation of this dish, and mine is an old family favourite that's been refined over the years. You could even add a bit of granola or muesli to this recipe and you've got a decadent breakfast dish too.

For the rhubarb, preheat the oven to 200°C and place a roasting pan in the oven to heat. Place a tray in the freezer.

Wash the rhubarb thoroughly, then use a small knife to peel and remove the fibrous skin. Cut into uniform 5 cm long batons. Toss in the sugar, then place in the hot pan in a single layer. Roast for 5–7 minutes until tender.

Transfer rhubarb to the tray that has been in the freezer. Place rhubarb in the freezer until completely chilled, but not frozen. Sprinkle rhubarb with the lime or lemon zest.

To make the custard, preheat the oven to 175°C. Place the cream, milk, vanilla bean and seeds in a saucepan and heat to 80°C (just below boiling point). Combine the egg yolks and sugar in a mixing bowl and whisk until pale and creamy. Pour the hot milk mixture over the yolk mixture, stirring gently to combine. Pass through a fine sieve into a deep baking tray (20 cm × 20 cm × 5 cm).

Bake for 40 minutes or until the top of the custard is golden and caramelised. Remove from the oven and leave to cool for 20–30 minutes, to warm room temperature. Transfer to a food processor and purée for 45 seconds on high, until smooth.

Meanwhile, make the oat biscuit, if using. Combine all the ingredients in a bowl. Transfer to a large baking tray lined with baking paper, and bake at 120°C until golden brown. Leave to cool for 15 minutes before serving.

To serve, spoon 2 tablespoons burnt custard onto each plate. Arrange rhubarb nicely on the custard and top with 2 teaspoons oat biscuit and freshly grated orange zest.

CHEF'S NOTE

Everybody likes their rhubarb cooked differently: some like it stewed until it's falling apart, whereas my preference is to have it just a fraction past al dente. In my opinion, perfectly cooked is with a little bit of texture and bite. Leaving it in the syrup is always a good idea too, as it keeps the rhubarb moist and juicy – if left in the fridge, it will last for a good couple of weeks.

TO DRINK

Whenever I think of rhubarb I think of ice wine made from the cabernet franc grape. This grape highlights the earthy character of rhubarb and made into an ice wine, the wine retains high natural acidity that is perfect for cutting the richness of the custard. Inniskillin winery based in Ontario, Canada produces an incredible ice wine from cabernet franc.

MY MARKET TIP

When sourcing rhubarb, try to find the reddest possible as it will be sweeter. Forced rhubarb is a great way to go if you can find it – this is the out-of-season variety that is grown indoors and has crimson stalks. Don't eat rhubarb leaves as they are toxic!

Mandarin and Lemon Verbena Cake, Mandarin Mascarpone

Bitter . Sweet . Spicy

SERVES 8

MANDARIN OLIVE OIL CAKE
300 g caster sugar
100 ground almonds
100 g panko breadcrumbs
1 teaspoon baking powder
6 juniper berries, toasted
    and ground
8 eggs
400 ml mandarin pressed
    olive oil
finely grated zest
    of 6 mandarins

VERBENA SYRUP
150 g caster sugar
100 ml mandarin juice
400 ml water
30 g lemon verbena leaves

MANDARIN MASCARPONE
250 g mascarpone
zest of 2 mandarins
pinch of salt

**CANDIED MANDARIN
(OPTIONAL)**
1 mandarin
200 ml sugar syrup

The fragrance of lemon verbena really is outstanding and it is one of my most used herbs from the garden. Whether in a cake like this one, or an ice-cream or sorbet, even in a cup of tea, it truly is delicious! If you can't find a mandarin-infused olive oil, extra virgin olive oil can be used in the cake instead.

To make the cake, preheat the oven to 165°C and line a 20 cm square cake tin with baking paper, extending over 2 sides.

Combine the dry ingredients in a mixing bowl. Using a stick blender, mix the eggs in another bowl until combined then with the blender running add the olive oil gradually until emulsified. Blend in the zest.

Mix the wet ingredients into the dry to make a runny batter. Pour into the prepared tin and bake for 45–60 minutes or until a skewer inserted into the middle of the cake comes out clean.

For the syrup, place the sugar, juice and water in a heavy-based saucepan over medium heat. Bring to the boil, stirring to dissolve the sugar. Cook until reduced and syrupy. Remove from the heat and add the lemon verbena. Set aside for 30 minutes for the flavour to infuse.

Brush the hot cake with the warm syrup, reserving some syrup for serving, and leave to cool in the tin for about 30 minutes. Lift the cake from the tin and place on a wire rack to cool completely.

To make the mandarin mascarpone, combine all the ingredients in a mixing bowl with a spatula. Store in the fridge until ready to serve.

To make the candied mandarin, peel the mandarin and use a sharp knife to remove the white pith from the peel, as it is quite bitter. Cut the peel into strips about 5 cm × 3 mm. Place the mandarin peel and the syrup in a saucepan and simmer on medium heat for 10 minutes. The trick is not to boil it; instead, cook it slowly and gently until it becomes translucent. Once cooked, strain the mandarin peel and leave to dry.

To serve, cut the cake into eight 2.5 cm slabs. Place on plates with 1 tablespoon mandarin mascarpone, a drizzle of the remaining verbena syrup and some candied mandarin if using.

CHEF'S NOTE
One of my secret tips here is to macerate the lemon cake with the syrup while still warm – it really does soak it up like a sponge!

TO DRINK
The citrus nature of this dessert calls out for some late-harvested or botrytised riesling. The high acid nature of the grape helps balance out the sweetness of the late-harvested fruit. Examples like Pegasus Bay Aria from North Canterbury in New Zealand display notes of candied citrus, honey and orange peel, while remaining fresh and vibrant without cloying the palate.

MARKET TIP
Smell the citrus you're buying! If it is fragrant then it's normally ripe and ready to eat. You could also substitute other citrus fruit in this recipe if you prefer lime or orange.

Lemon Posset, Rhubarb and Rose Compote

Sour . Bitter . Sweet . Temperature

SERVES 8

LEMON POSSET
1.2 litres thickened cream
350 g caster sugar
strips of peel from 5 lemons
150 ml lemon juice

RHUBARB AND ROSE COMPOTE
500 g rhubarb, washed, trimmed
   and cut into 2–3 cm pieces
110 g raw sugar
finely grated zest and juice
   of ½ orange
¼ cup water
1–2 teaspoons rosewater
westringia leaves, rosemary
   flowers or basil buds,
   to garnish (optional)

A very simple recipe that achieves great results, a posset is pretty much just thickened cream normally flavoured with lemon. It's a really tasty dessert that takes no time at all and is lovely to bring to the table individually in pretty serving glasses.

To make the lemon posset, place the cream in a medium saucepan and bring to the boil. Remove from the heat and stir in the sugar, lemon peel and juice. Return to the boil and simmer for 1 minute. Remove from the heat, pass through a fine sieve into a bowl and allow to cool for 15 minutes. Pour into eight 150 ml capacity serving glasses. Leave to cool completely before putting in the fridge to set for 4–6 hours.

For the rhubarb and rose compote, combine the rhubarb and sugar in a large saucepan off the heat. Stand for 10–15 minutes, until the sugar draws out some of the liquid. Add the orange zest, juice and water. Bring to the boil, stirring occasionally. Reduce the heat to low and simmer for about 5 minutes, until the rhubarb has broken down but some pieces remain whole. Remove from the heat and stir in the rosewater. Leave to cool. The compote will keep for up to 4 days in an airtight container in the fridge.

To serve, take the possets from the fridge just before serving. Spoon the rhubarb compote on top of the possets, making sure to leave clean edges on the glass. Garnish each glass with a few westringia leaves, rosemary flowers or basil buds, if you wish.

CHEF'S NOTE
You can add another dimension to this dish by combining subtle flavours that work well with the lemon: vanilla, cinnamon or even infusing herbs such as lemon thyme or lemon verbena. Westringia is a member of the mint family and is commonly grown in gardens as a shrub or hedge.

TO DRINK
A very aromatic and light sweet wine is my choice for this dessert. Perhaps a viognier, which will show floral aromas – the rose from the dish and its low sweetness perfectly marries with the texture of the posset. There are beautiful wines produced all around the world from this grape. Choose a naturally sweet late-harvest style here.

MARKET TIP
If you're not a rhubarb fan, then other stewed or poached fruit is a nice garnish with the posset. Even a jelly on top is a great little touch that elevates the posset to the next level.

Blueberries, Yoghurt, Rosemary Apple Granita

SERVES 4–6

YOGHURT
250 g yoghurt
50 g icing sugar, or more
   to taste, sifted
finely grated zest and juice
   (to taste) of ½ lemon
small pinch of salt

ROSEMARY APPLE GRANITA
150 ml store-bought
   apple juice
50 ml water
20 g caster sugar
½ tablespoon rosemary leaves
1 gelatine leaf (gold strength)

BLUEBERRY COMPOTE
50 g caster sugar
25 g liquid glucose
50 ml water
200 g frozen blueberries
finely grated zest and juice of
   ½ lime
50 g fresh blueberries,
   to serve

In the restaurants we are always looking for new and different things, interesting combinations and things to excite. And that's exactly what this dish is: who would think rosemary would be great in a dessert? The fragrance and savoury tones of the rosemary make this an unusual yet tasty way to finish a meal.

To prepare the yoghurt, line a colander with cheesecloth and spoon the yoghurt into it. Sit the colander over a bowl to drain. Twist the cheesecloth at the top to close, and refrigerate overnight. The whey will drain into the bowl, leaving behind a thicker, creamier yoghurt.

Next day, whisk the icing sugar, zest and salt into the drained yoghurt, then add lemon juice to taste.

To make the granita, combine the apple juice, water, caster sugar and rosemary leaves in a medium saucepan. Stir over medium–low heat to dissolve the sugar, then bring to the boil. Remove from the heat and set aside to infuse for 5 minutes.

Meanwhile, place the gelatine leaf in a bowl of iced water for 5 minutes to soften. Squeeze excess water from the gelatine, add to the apple juice mixture and stir to dissolve. Strain into a chilled shallow tray (non-aluminium) and place in the freezer. Leave to freeze for 2 hours, then scrape the granita with a fork every hour or so for 4 hours to make a coarse, crystallised consistency.

To make the compote, combine the sugar, glucose and water in a large saucepan. Stir over low heat until the glucose and sugar have dissolved. Increase the heat to high, and when it reaches 120°C on a sugar thermometer, add the frozen blueberries. Cook for 15 minutes, then strain. Set the blueberries aside. Return the liquid to the saucepan on a high heat and once the mixture reaches 110°C on a sugar thermometer, add the lime juice. Remove from the heat and leave to cool.

When the blueberries and the liquid have both cooled to room temperature, combine them in a bowl and stir in the zest. If not using straight away, cover and keep in the fridge for up to 3 days.

To serve, in small bowls scoop 2 tablespoons yoghurt with 2 tablespoons compote alongside and add a few fresh blueberries on top. Finish with 2 generous teaspoons of granita. Garnish with a few rosemary flowers to make it look extra special, if you wish.

CHEF'S NOTE

This is an interesting and refreshing dessert that can be prepared ahead. It's even nice to garnish with the rosemary flowers if you can find some.

TO DRINK

In Piedmonte in north-west Italy, there is a sweet red wine made from the brachetto grape. The wines of Brachetto d'Acqui are light and refreshingly sweet. They almost always taste like a mixture of blueberries and ripe strawberries while the 'frizzante' nature of the wine leaves your palate feeling refreshed. A perfect wine for a light and refreshing berry dessert.

MARKET TIP

Blueberries come into season in late spring. If making this dessert out of season, you can simply leave out the fresh berries on the top.

Andy's Tiramisu

SERVES 8

BISCUIT DE SAVOIE
5 eggs, separated
160 g icing sugar
130 g plain flour
2 tablespoons cornflour

TIRAMISU
400 ml strong freshly
    brewed coffee
150 ml marsala
    (or a coffee liqueur)
4 eggs, separated
finely grated zest of 1 orange
100 g caster sugar
200 ml thickened cream
400 g mascarpone
cocoa powder, for dusting

I'm not sure if there is a more famous Italian dessert than tiramisu. Great for entertaining and the beauty is that this dish is best made the day before, in a great big bowl and just scooped directly onto the plate. Heaven!

To make the biscuits, preheat the oven to 180°C and line 2 large baking trays with baking paper. Place the egg yolks and half the sugar in a heatproof mixing bowl over a saucepan of gently simmering water (make sure the base of the bowl doesn't touch the water). Use electric beaters to beat until the mixture is thick and forms a ribbon when drizzled back over itself. Fold in the sifted flours.

Use clean beaters to beat the egg whites until soft peaks form. Gradually add the remaining sugar, beating constantly, to make a meringue mixture. Fold the meringue into the yolk mixture, then transfer to a piping bag fitted with a plain 1.5 cm nozzle. Pipe into fingers about 10 cm long and 3 cm wide, or discs about 15 cm in diameter. Bake for 15–18 minutes, until lightly golden. Transfer to a wire rack to cool.

For the tiramisu, combine the coffee and marsala in a bowl and set aside. Place the egg yolks, zest and half the sugar in a heatproof bowl over a saucepan of gently simmering water and beat to ribbon stage (as for the biscuit mixture above). Transfer to a cool bowl, on a stand mixer if you like, and beat for about 5 minutes, until pale, thick and cool.

Use a balloon whisk to semi-whip the cream (until thickened but not forming peaks), and stir the mascarpone to loosen. Fold into the yolk mixture. Beat the egg whites until soft peaks form, then gradually add the remaining sugar, beating constantly until combined. Using a spatula, fold the meringue into the mascarpone mixture.

To assemble, dip a biscuit into the coffee mixture until soft and place into the base of an 18 cm diameter (8-cup capacity) serving bowl or dish. Repeat with soaked biscuits to cover the base.

Cover the biscuits with a layer of the mascarpone mixture, then add another layer of soaked biscuits.

Repeat 2 or 3 times depending on the proportions of your bowl. Cover and refrigerate overnight, or at least 2–3 hours for the flavours to develop. Dust with cocoa and serve.

CHEF'S NOTE

It's always better if you can make the biscuits yourself for this one, but if you're time poor, there are some store bought *biscuit de savoie* or lady fingers available that are pretty good too.

TO DRINK

The classic match would be a rich and sweet marsala from Sicily. However, if this is not an easy find then look to Rutherglen topaque as an alternative. The rich and developed wood and raisin notes in the wine are perfectly suited to the flavours of tiramisu. Vin santo wines from Tuscany would also complement this classic dessert.

MARKET TIP

Coffee! The key to a tiramisu is the coffee. If you can, brew your own using the best beans you can find and make it super strong. The mascarpone and the biscuits soak it all up for an end result that is pretty much perfect!

Spring Heroes

Peas.

   As far as a match of season and ingredients go, is there anything that identifies a time of year more than peas do for spring? Spring peas: sweet little green jewels that pop with flavour and are even a special treat eaten raw, freshly popped from their protective cocoon. Perfect for salads, risotto, chilled or warm soups, a dressing or vinaigrette, as the star of the show using different varietals or as a perfect accompaniment to a slow-roasted lamb shoulder. Married with fresh mint, feta, basil, champagne vinegar and sea salt, let them shine and enjoy the springtime.

Rhubarb.

   My grandmother used to grow rhubarb in the backyard and one of my fondest memories from childhood is Audrey's stewed rhubarb and custard. If we'd behaved (which wasn't that often, to be honest) then we had the option of ice-cream. She never added too much sugar, and the sharpness of the fruit is without doubt the one thing that really reminds me of her tart red compote. On occasion it would make its way to join some apples and pears for the perfect crumble, a natural end to her slow-roasted leg of lamb and all the trimmings. These days in the restaurants we use rhubarb in many different forms. It may be gently poached or cooked sous vide, thinly sliced raw to add some zing and extra acid to a heavy protein, puree or gel, even dried into chips. We look to counterbalance the fat and sweetness in some dishes with the astringent flavour profiles that rhubarb has to offer, but regardless of the exploration that experience allows me in a professional sense, sometimes I still just yearn for Nan's stewed rhubarb and custard.

Spring Menu I

STARTER

Smoked Ham Hock and Pea Soup,
Mint Crème Fraîche

(page 24)

MAIN

Roasted Leg of Lamb,
Rainbow Chard, Sauce Paloise

(page 32)

SIDE

Globe Artichokes, Saffron, Shallots

(page 43)

DESSERT

Lemon Posset, Rhubarb and Rose Compote

(page 50)

Spring Menu 2

STARTER

Cured Wagyu, Borlotti Beans, Sherry Vinegar

(page 26)

MAIN

Roast Duck, Turnips, Blood Orange

(page 34)

SIDES

Charred Corn, Green Chilli, Lime

(page 44)

Duck Fat Roasted Potatoes, Herb Salt

(page 40)

DESSERT

Blueberries, Yoghurt, Rosemary Apple Granita

(page 52)

CURED WAGYU, BORLOTTI BEANS,
SHERRY VINEGAR   (PAGE 26)

BLUEBERRIES, YOGHURT, ROSEMARY
APPLE GRANITA   (PAGE 52)

ROAST DUCK, TURNIPS, BLOOD
ORANGE   (PAGE 34)

Summer

The heat of a true Aussie summer really is one
of the finest, yet most extreme, environments I've ever
experienced. Luckily for me I live in Melbourne, where
the temperature still reaches 40 degrees at its peak,
but tends to be slightly more manageable than in other
parts of the country.

Childhood memories of sun, surf, snags, sand and
sunburn fill my mind with a warm glow that's truly only
matched by the fierce summer sun itself. Playing beach
cricket with my brother, swimming and snorkelling
for abalone with my dad, fishing in the local bay for
flathead and snapper, and warm nights spent outside
cooking on the old Aussie barbecue.

And, while the weather itself dictates what we eat
during these months, of course the produce does
too. The true fruits of summer – berries, cherries,
figs, mangoes and peaches, served simply with a
wonderful ice-cream or poached gently in an aromatic
and sugary syrup. The tomatoes and zucchini flowers
that make a perfect match for local olive oil, sea salt
and basil . . . Simple salads to enjoy outdoors with an
abundance of seafood, or grilled meats for a hot balmy
night. God bless Australia, I love her and her summer!

Hiramasa Kingfish, Finger Lime, White Soy

Salty . Umami . Sour

SERVES 8

1 × 750 g–1 kg kingfish fillet
3 finger limes
50 ml white soy sauce
50 ml extra virgin olive oil
2 teaspoons mirin
1 spring onion, thinly
   sliced diagonally
1 tablespoon sesame
   seeds, toasted
coriander, to garnish

CURE
500 g fine salt
250 g sugar
finely grated zest of 1 lemon
finely grated zest of 1 orange

Hiramasa kingfish or yellowtail kingfish is a wonderful sustainable fish that has become rather trendy and widely used in Australia over the last few years. Its high fat content makes it perfect to serve raw, sashimi-style, or lightly cured with sea salt and sugar. It's highly regarded in Japan, so with this influence I've combined some white soy with a touch of Australiana, using the native finger lime. If you can't find finger limes, you can use any citrus – the best options are grapefruit, limes and lemons, juiced or chopped into small segments.

For the cure, combine the ingredients in a bowl and set aside. Remove any bloodlines, sinew and pin bones from the fillet.

Spread half the cure mixture over a glass or ceramic dish (with a deep rim) and sit the fish on it. Cover the fish with the remaining mixture. Cover and place in the fridge for 1 hour to cure.

Remove the fish from the curing mixture and wash off any excess. Pat dry with a clean cloth. Rest the cleaned fish in the fridge for 1 more hour.

Halve the finger limes and gently squeeze out the little beads inside. Discard any seeds. In a small bowl, combine the white soy sauce, olive oil, mirin and finger lime flesh. Add the spring onion and sesame seeds to the vinaigrette.

Thinly slice the kingfish into clean smooth pieces using the whole length of the knife. Dress the kingfish with the soy vinaigrette and garnish with coriander. Serve immediately.

CHEF'S NOTE

Kingfish is my go-to fish these days for serving raw, but there are many suitable replacements if you want to mix it up. King or Atlantic salmon, yellowfin tuna, snapper or mackerel all work fine too. Just choose one to suit your tastes and budget. When preparing, work in a clean and hygienic manner, using a razor-sharp knife when slicing to ensure best results.

TO DRINK

The acidity of the finger lime for me calls for a vibrant white wine with enough volume to marry the delicate flesh of the kingfish while not forgetting a savoury touch to mirror the white soy. I would team this with a white Bordeaux blend from its native region with a limited amount of oak.

MARKET TIP

When serving fish raw, you need to make sure you buy the freshest fish possible and handle it correctly. It's best to buy and serve on the same day, and keep it refrigerated until just before serving. White soy sauce is available from specialty Asian grocery shops.

Grilled Calamari, Preserved Lemon Gremolata

Texture . Bitter . Salty

SERVES 6

2 × 500 g calamari, cleaned and
    patted dry (see Chef's Note)
olive oil, to drizzle
sea salt
extra virgin olive oil, to dress
mint and parsley leaves,
    to finish
lemon wedges, to serve

PRESERVED LEMON
GREMOLATA
100 g panko breadcrumbs
¼ preserved lemon,
    flesh only, diced
finely grated zest of 1 lemon
1 bunch flat-leaf parsley,
    leaves finely sliced
2 teaspoons capers, rinsed
    and drained
pinch of cayenne pepper
sea salt, to season

One European summer I was lucky enough to work on a super yacht, where we travelled the Greek islands for a couple of months. This was where I really enjoyed fresh calamari or squid, straight from the ocean, served simply with lemon and herbs. This dish takes its inspiration from that long-ago summer, and jazzes it up with preserved lemon and a lovely herby salsa.

Preheat the oven to 160°C. To make the gremolata, spread the breadcrumbs on a baking tray and toast in the oven for about 10–15 minutes or until golden. Transfer to a plate to cool. Meanwhile, preheat a barbecue grillplate on high heat.

Combine the toasted breadcrumbs, preserved lemon, lemon zest, parsley and capers in a bowl. Season with cayenne pepper and salt.

Drizzle the calamari with olive oil and season with salt. Place directly on the barbecue grillplate and cook on one side for 2 minutes, then turn and cook for 1 minute more. Remove from barbecue and slice into 5 equal pieces each.

Place on serving plates or a platter, dress with extra virgin olive oil and scatter generously with the gremolata. Garnish with mint and parsley leaves, and serve with lemon wedges.

CHEF'S NOTE

To clean calamari, I start by cutting the tentacles at the top of the head. I then carefully remove the insides, trying not to break the ink sack, or else it gets messy! Then I remove the wings. Next I peel the membrane off the body itself, and then from the wings. This breaks the calamari down into its main parts, and it's ready for me to cut and portion however I wish.

TO DRINK

To control the ardour of the garlic and to marry the calamari texture I would choose a white wine from the Loire Valley, kingdom of the chenin blanc. A wine from Anjou would be my pick here.

MARKET TIP

Always use fresh calamari! Frozen stuff just isn't the same, and lots of people have a bad memory of rubbery or chewy calamari. There are only really two reasons: either it's overcooked or an inferior frozen product. Sometimes you can even find calamari that has been cleaned and prepared already from your fishmonger, a real luxury.

Vitello Tonnato

SERVES 8

POACHED VEAL

2 tablespoons vegetable oil
1 × 1–1.2 kg veal girello or eye
    of round
sea salt
freshly ground black pepper
1 carrot, chopped
1 celery stick, chopped
1 onion, chopped
8 black peppercorns
4 cloves
100 ml white-wine vinegar
250 ml white wine
2 bay leaves
1 sprig thyme
1 sprig rosemary
3 anchovies
zest of 1 lemon

TUNA SAUCE

3 hard-boiled eggs (about
    7–8 minutes cooking time)
200 g confit tuna (or drained
    canned tuna in oil)
3 anchovies
1 tablespoon capers in brine,
    rinsed and drained
juice of 1 lemon
150 ml olive oil
sea salt
freshly ground black pepper
splash of Tabasco
splash of Worcestershire sauce

GARNISH

1 tablespoon capers, fried
    (see page 84)
10 anchovies, split
20 flat-leaf parsley leaves
2 teaspoons extra virgin
    olive oil
large handful of rocket leaves
¼ cup parmesan shavings

An absolute classic Piedmontese dish of poached veal and
a creamy, mayonnaise-style sauce made with tuna, vitello
tonnato really is one of my favorite things to eat in summer.
Don't be scared by the veal, or the fact it's cold: when you
have a proper serve of this, it will make you come back for
more, time and time again!

For the poached veal, heat the oil in a large heavy-based saucepan over
high heat. Season the veal with salt and pepper and briefly sear on all
sides, turning occasionally, until golden. Remove and set aside. Reduce
heat to medium.

Add the vegetables, peppercorns and cloves. Sauté until the
vegetables are tender but not coloured. Add the vinegar and cook until
reduced by half, then add the wine and cook until reduced by half.

Return the veal to the pan, add the herbs, anchovies and zest and
just cover with water. Bring to a simmer (don't boil), then reduce the
heat to very low and poach gently for 10–15 minutes, until the veal is just
a little bit under-cooked. Remove from the heat and set aside to cool
in the cooking liquid. (The meat will feel rare to medium–rare but will
have cooked perfectly in the residual heat as it cools.) When cool,
remove the veal from the liquid.

Meanwhile, to make the tuna sauce, peel the eggs and place in a food
processor with the tuna, anchovies, capers and lemon juice. Process
until smooth. With the motor running, gradually add the olive oil to make
a lovely thick emulsion. If you think it is too thick you can always add
a little warm water to adjust the consistency. Season to taste with salt,
pepper, Tabasco and Worcestershire sauce.

To serve, thinly slice the veal and arrange nicely on a plate. Drizzle
with the tuna sauce – sometimes I like to make layers, so it is veal/sauce/
veal/sauce. Garnish with fried capers, anchovies, parsley, rocket and
parmesan shavings. Drizzle with olive oil and finish with salt and pepper.

CHEF'S NOTE

Any leftover tuna mayonnaise is great
in sandwiches, used as a spread or
sometimes I even serve it as a dip with
crackers and croutons. It keeps for a few
days in the fridge and is also great to
serve with grilled fish and a slice of lemon.

TO DRINK

What better than a regional match for an
iconic dish. My choice is an arneis from the
Piedmonte in northern Italy. Choose a more
textural arneis to match the generosity of
this dish or alternatively pair it with a light
red such as a blaufränkisch from Austria
or an unoaked barbera from Alba.

MARKET TIP

'Girello' is my favourite cut for this dish.
Eye of round, or 'veal roast', is a great
cut too, but you can also use the topside
or the silverside. Ask your butcher for
advice about these cuts if you are not
sure. If you're not a fan of veal, then you
could always substitute pork in the recipe.
Loin or fillet would work best.

Zucchini Flowers, Piperade, Basil

SERVES 4

8 zucchini flowers
250 g ricotta
sea salt
freshly ground black pepper
extra virgin olive oil and basil
    leaves, to serve

PIPERADE
140 g pancetta, finely chopped
1 red onion, finely chopped
1 green capsicum, sliced
1 yellow capsicum sliced
1 red capsicum, sliced
4 padron or small green
    chillies, seeded and sliced
2 tablespoons tomato paste
500 g tomatoes, chopped
sea salt, to season
few basil leaves,
    finely shredded

A lot more common and readily available than ever before, zucchini flowers let me know that summer has truly arrived. They are a fantastic 'vehicle' for filling with a seafood mousse or a soft cheese such as ricotta or a goat's curd. They can be steamed or dipped in a light batter and fried, or simply warmed in a pan of olive oil to garnish a summer salad and take it to the next level.

To make the piperade, preheat a wide medium pan over medium–high heat. Add the pancetta and cook until golden brown and the fat has rendered. Use a slotted spoon to remove the pancetta from the pan and strain off all but about 1 tablespoon of the fat. Reserve the pancetta and fat separately.

Reheat the pan over medium heat. Add the onion and cook until soft but not coloured, then add the capsicum and chilli and keep cooking until soft, again without browning. Add the tomato paste and cook, stirring, for about 2 minutes. Stir in the chopped tomato and return the pancetta to the pan. Cook, stirring occasionally, until the sauce reduces and thickens. Season with salt and stir in the basil, and if you like you can add the pancetta fat back to the pan for extra flavour.

Remove the stamens and stalk ends from the zucchini flowers. Season the ricotta with salt and pepper and mash until softened. Spoon the ricotta into each zucchini flower and gently press back into shape. My little trick is to wrap the flowers in plastic film to protect them while steaming or poaching: wrap the zucchini flower snugly, then knot both ends. Repeat with every flower. Place in a large steamer in a single layer and cook for 8–10 minutes, until heated through.

To serve, spread warm piperade on the base of each serving plate and arrange the flowers on top. Drizzle with olive oil and garnish with basil.

CHEF'S NOTE

It's important when preparing the flower to be filled that you hold it carefully in your hand and then gently blow into it, and it will open nicely allowing you to remove the stamen. Once removed, you can stuff the flower with your desired filling.

TO DRINK

A white wine from Provence along the coast in the south of France, with character built by the warm summer and limestone soil, will express its character with the piperade and show beautiful complexity to pair with the zucchini flower.

MARKET TIP

Did you know it's the female zucchini flowers that have a thicker, wider base? They're the ones you would have normally seen as it's the female that develops into the fruit that we eat – the male only has a short little stem. The male has a single stamen in the centre of the flower, while the female flower has a more complex stigma.

Venison Tartare, Pine Nuts, Buckwheat Crackers

SERVES 4

sea salt
freshly ground pepper

BUCKWHEAT CRACKERS
200 g buckwheat
sea salt
700 g day-old sourdough
   bread, torn
1 litre water
grapeseed oil, to deep-fry

VENISON TARTARE
400 g venison loin, cleaned,
   finely diced
2 roasted red capsicums,
   finely diced
30 ml extra virgin olive oil
1 tablespoon red-wine vinegar
1 golden shallot, finely diced
½ bunch chives, finely chopped
splash of Tabasco
pinch of cayenne pepper
⅓ cup pine nuts, toasted

While raw meat can be a bit scary and intimidating for some, it's a wonderful way to enjoy the texture and flavour of different meats. Adding a bit of spice is always great too. With every dish we are looking for balance in flavour and a textural element to really bring it together, and the buckwheat crackers and the pine nuts do the textural work here.

To make the crackers, place the buckwheat in a large saucepan, cover with cold water and add a pinch of salt. Cook for 20–25 minutes, until tender. Drain well and rinse in cold water to remove the starch.

Cook the sourdough in the 1 litre water on a low heat until completely soft, then drain off any excess water.

Process the sourdough in a food processor until smooth, then transfer to a bowl and fold in the buckwheat.

Preheat the oven to 50°C. Roll the mixture evenly between 2 sheets of baking paper until 3 mm thick. Lay out on a baking tray, remove the top layer of baking paper and place in the oven to dehydrate for 3 hours until just dry. Be careful that it doesn't become too dry or it won't puff when fried.

Pour enough oil into a large saucepan so it is just under half full. Heat over medium–high heat to 200°C. Break the cracker sheets into pieces approximately 6 cm × 6 cm and deep-fry until puffed and golden. Drain on paper towel and season with salt.

For the venison tartare, combine all the ingredients in a bowl and mix well. Season to taste with salt and pepper. If you like it a little spicy, add some more Tabasco and cayenne pepper.

Divide the tartare mixture between plates and serve with the crackers.

CHEF'S NOTE

This recipe works really well with other meats too: grass-fed beef, veal or even lamb. And you don't need to be restricted to using a primary cut like the loin or fillet; a leg muscle, say, the rump or rump cap, is great. Even topside, so long as you clean and remove all the sinew and fat and dice or mince it nice and finely.

TO DRINK

Carignan or grenache from a warm region. These are juicy and generous, showing spices and fruit to marry with the texture and condiment. The rustic flavours of the wine will complement the gamey flavours of the venison.

MARKET TIP

Roasted capsicum, or roasted red peppers as I like to call them, are easy to do and keep well in the fridge in olive oil for a week or longer. Of course, you can also buy them ready-prepared if you're time poor and want a convenient product, but it's always handy to have a jar in the fridge to use in simple salads or on a piece of nice crusty bread with goat's cheese and fresh basil!

Wagyu Brochettes, Ratatouille Vegetables

MAKES 10

1 × 1 kg wagyu rump, cut
    into large pieces about
    4 cm square
2 tomatoes
1 eggplant
1 green zucchini
1 yellow zucchini
2 red onions
1 yellow capsicum
1 red capsicum
1 green capsicum

MARINADE

2 cloves garlic, finely chopped
100 ml grapeseed oil
1 sprig thyme
1 sprig rosemary
¼ cup soy sauce
2 tablespoons honey
2 tablespoons tomato sauce
1 tablespoon
    Worcestershire sauce
25 ml red-wine vinegar
sea salt, to season
freshly ground black pepper,
    to season

What's better than a homemade shashlik or kebab cooked on the barbecue? If you use good-quality meat, and baste it during cooking, the results are not only eye-catching, they are delicious too. Using the wonderful summer vegetables in season – tomato, zucchini, eggplant, capsicum and red onion – this can be a meal on its own, or a centrepiece for the glamorous Aussie barbecue.

To make the marinade, place all the ingredients in a large bowl, season with salt and pepper and mix thoroughly.

Toss the diced beef with half of the marinade in a large bowl, then cover and put in the fridge overnight. Refrigerate the remaining marinade separately.

Next day, soak ten bamboo skewers in water for 30 minutes. Cut all the vegetables into large squares or diamonds, about the same size as the beef. Then thread the beef onto the skewers, alternating with different vegetables, and making sure you mix up the colours.

Divide the remaining marinade between two small bowls. Preheat a barbecue grillplate to high heat. Brush the brochettes with marinade from one of the bowls. Cook the brochettes on the barbecue for about 3–4 minutes each side for medium–rare. Baste with the leftover marinade during cooking. Set aside to rest for 5–10 minutes.

Brush with marinade from the second bowl before serving. Serve with wedges of iceberg lettuce and crème fraîche dressing or with Charred Cos, Caper, Anchovy, Chives (page 84).

CHEF'S NOTE

If you marinate the meat first overnight before putting it on the skewer, it helps to tenderise the meat and develops a wonderful flavour. Marinate it for 3 hours, as a minimum, if you're not able to start it the day before.

TO DRINK

Tempranillo. Juicy and charming, this grape variety shows a great result aged in a bit of American oak as this adds sweet and smoky flavours to the characteristic dark berries. The tannins will build just enough texture to stand with the beef. The kingdom of this grape variety is Rioja, in Spain.

MARKET TIP

I use wagyu for this recipe because it has a high fat content and a wonderful flavour, but you don't need to use eye fillet for this one. A good 'secondary cut' like rump or topside is perfect, and if wagyu doesn't fit into your budget, then a really good grass-fed product works well too.

Yellowfin Tuna, Broad Beans, Coriander

SUMMER

MAIN

SERVES 6

1 × 750 g piece yellowfin tuna,
    at room temperature
olive oil, to brush
sea salt
1 lemon, cut into wedges

DRAGONCELLO DRESSING

3 slices ciabatta or sourdough,
    crusts removed
2½ tablespoons red-wine
    vinegar
40 g coriander leaves
40 g tarragon leaves
40 g parsley leaves
2 anchovies
300 ml olive oil
100 g broad beans, shelled
    and cooked
100 g peas, shelled and cooked
2 tablespoons chopped
    coriander, extra

One of the most versatile fish available, tuna is great raw, just cooked or even confit (although personally I avoid tinned, unless it's for the kids' lunchboxes!). Tuna marries really well with red-wine vinegar, and is a meaty kind of fish that can handle bold flavours.

To make the dressing, soak the bread in the vinegar until it is soft and moist, then squeeze out any excess liquid.

Blitz the soaked bread, herbs, anchovies and oil in a blender until smooth. Season to taste and add a little more vinegar if more acidity is required. Strain through a fine sieve into a bowl and stand over a larger bowl of ice to cool if it has heated up a touch in the blender. This ensures the dressing stays green and vibrant.

Preheat a barbecue grillplate on high heat. Brush the fish generously with olive oil and season well with salt. Cook on the barbecue for 2–3 minutes each side. Remove from the grill. The tuna should be well caramelised on the outside and super-rare in the middle.

Place broad beans and peas in a bowl, add the extra coriander and 100 ml of the dressing. Toss to combine. Carve the tuna into 6 steaks and serve drizzled with the remaining dressing and a few flakes of sea salt.

CHEF'S NOTE

Fresh tuna should be cooked medium-rare or rare and served with a simple garnish that is high in acid to cut through the fattiness of the fish itself, showcasing the quality and freshness of the fish.

TO DRINK

A red wine with a great expression of a limestone terroir is perfect here, my choice being something from Saint Aubin, south of Burgundy – a straight pinot noir. A crunchy fruit-forward style with a freshness enhanced by firm and thin, elegant tannins adds intensity and energy to the match.

MARKET TIP

Be sure to source a beautiful piece of tuna, deep red, firm and from the centre of the fish if possible, ensuring you have little sinew and waste. Ask the fishmonger to remove the skin and any blood line so all you have to do is cook it. Try to buy and cook on the same day.

Southern Rock Lobster, Sauce Bois Boudran

Sweet . Sour . Spicy

SUMMER

MAIN

SERVES 4–6

2 × 600 g southern
  rock lobsters
stalks from ¼ bunch tarragon
sea salt
50 ml olive oil
1 lemon, halved
green salad, to serve

SAUCE BOIS BOUDRAN
300 ml olive oil
200 ml tomato sauce (ketchup)
1½ tablespoons finely diced
  golden shallots
1 tablespoon sherry vinegar
3 teaspoons Dijon mustard
3 teaspoons
  Worcestershire sauce
½ teaspoon Tabasco
2 teaspoons chopped chives
2 teaspoons chopped tarragon

An expensive crustacean that I really do keep for a special occasion or birthday treat, the southern rock lobster's juicy, firm white and red flesh is a true Aussie delicacy. In this dish I serve it with a classic sauce called bois boudran: a wonderful blend of tomatoes, mustard and one of my favourite herbs, tarragon. Once you taste the bois boudran you will fall in love with it and find any excuse to dress a piece of grilled fish or poached chicken with it.

Place the lobsters in the freezer for 30 minutes. To make the sauce, combine all the ingredients in a bowl and mix well. Set aside.

Place a pot of water big enough to hold the lobsters over high heat and bring to the boil with the tarragon stalks and a generous pinch of salt. Meanwhile, preheat a barbecue grillplate on medium–high heat and prepare a large bowl of iced water.

Remove the lobsters from the freezer. Using the tip of a small sharp knife, pierce straight down behind the eyes. Add the lobsters to the pot, return to a simmer and cook for 5 minutes. Remove each lobster and allow the water to drain off, then plunge into the iced water to stop the cooking. Drain well.

Use a large sharp knife to split each lobster straight down the middle from head to tail so you have neat halves. Clean out the digestive tract. Brush each cut side liberally with olive oil and season with salt.

Place the lobsters on the barbecue flesh-side down. Cook for 4–5 minutes, until well charred, then turn and cook on the shell side for 4–5 minutes. Be sure to brush the flesh with olive oil during cooking. Squeeze the lemon juice all over the flesh before removing the lobsters from the barbecue.

Serve the lobsters hot, with the sauce on the side.

CHEF'S NOTE

Crays, crayfish or lobster? Depends who you ask I suppose . . . The correct term for the *Jasus edwardsii* is actually the southern rock lobster, but if you were to ask my nan, she would always order a 'big crayfish' for her birthday treat!

TO DRINK

The generous flesh and delicate flavours of the lobster here would be well supported by a white with volume and a lean palate. A marsanne roussane is a great blend, originally from a few appellations in the Rhône Valley, and there are also some amazing examples in South Australia and in California in the Santa Barbara region.

MARKET TIP

Try and buy live lobsters if you can, not frozen or pre-cooked. That way you will have the freshest and tastiest seafood when you're spending a fair amount of money on a premium product.

Whole Flounder Grenobloise

Texture . Sour . Salty

SERVES 4

2 × 500 g whole flounder,
   tail and wings trimmed
sea salt
freshly ground black pepper
plain flour, to dust
2 tablespoons olive oil
40 g butter, diced
1 lemon, flesh segmented
   and diced
2 teaspoons capers, rinsed
   and drained
2 teaspoons chopped flat-leaf
   parsley leaves
100 g croutons

'Grenobloise' is a classic French preparation, meaning literally from the town of Grenoble in south-east France. It's really just a sauce of brown butter, capers, parsley, lemon and croutons, perfect for a whole flat fish like flounder.

Preheat the oven to 180°C. Preheat a flameproof roasting pan on the stovetop over medium–high heat. Season the fish well with salt and pepper, and lightly flour both sides. Heat the oil in the pan, then add the fish (presentation side down) and cook until lightly browned. Turn and brown the other side. Transfer the pan to the oven and cook for 6–8 minutes, until the fish is just tender (the flesh will flake when tested with the tip of a knife).

Place the pan back on the stove over medium heat. Add the butter and let it gently foam. When the butter smells nutty add the lemon, capers and parsley.

Remove the fish from the pan and place on a serving plate. Spoon the butter mixture over the fish.

This sauce is also delicious served with the Charred Cos, Caper, Anchovy, Chives (page 84).

CHEF'S NOTE

I don't only use lemon juice in this recipe because it's always nice to have some segments or pieces of lemon too. And if you're feeling adventurous, try lime or even ruby red grapefruit to mix it up a bit.

TO DRINK

A cool climate chardonnay here, to keep the vivacity mirroring the acidity of the dressing when the richness of the butter is complemented by the volume of the wine. Light oak influence and freshness direct my choice to a Tasmanian chardonnay, more likely from the southern regions.

MARKET TIP

Though this sauce and garnish is perfect for flounder, it also goes really well with whiting, flathead or even salmon.

Slow-roasted Pork Shoulder, Lemon Thyme, Garlic

Umami . Salty . Bitter

SERVES 8–10

1 × 3–4 kg bone-in free-range
   pork shoulder
1 bulb garlic, cloves peeled
½ bunch lemon thyme
100 ml extra virgin olive oil
2 tablespoons sea salt

Roast pork is one of my favourite things to both cook and eat. Crispy crackling, juicy fatty meat . . . nothing beats it! On Christmas Day most years I have it as my centrepiece of a wonderful celebration lunch. The best thing about this recipe is that I cook it slowly overnight, so on Chrissy morning you don't have much to do except open presents and finish the last preparations for the lunch feast.

Place the pork skin-side up on a rimmed tray and leave uncovered in the fridge overnight so the skin dries out a little bit.

Preheat the oven to 220°C. Make a few incisions in the pork about 3 cm deep – enough to fit a garlic clove. Place garlic cloves in incisions, along with the lemon thyme. Rub all over with the olive oil and sprinkle with the salt.

Place the pork on a rack in a roasting pan. Roast for 20–30 minutes, until the skin has crackled and puffed. Reduce the temperature to 80°C and cook for 8–10 hours (it's a bit like a confit process).

Remove from the oven and rest for about 1 hour.

To serve, place the pork back into a 200°C for 10–15 minutes to reheat. Remove the crackled skin and cut it into pieces. Carve the meat from the bone.

CHEF'S NOTE

Make sure that you leave the pork shoulder uncovered for at least 12 hours to let the skin dry out before cooking. This, plus a good rub of olive oil and a decent sprinkle of salt, helps get the crackling even crispier!

TO DRINK

Nothing is better than the crunchy red berry flavours of a gamay, served just below cellar temperature (around 14 degrees). Great examples have started appearing in Australia, especially from the north-eastern part of Victoria.

MARKET TIP

If you can afford it, buy really good-quality free-range pork. The flavour difference compared to the regular stuff will astound you, and the creaminess of the fat makes for a delicious and juicy end result.

Quinoa, Cucumber, Radish, Avocado

SERVES 6

2 cups red quinoa
1 litre water
5 juniper berries
1 bay leaf
25 g salt
extra virgin olive oil, to drizzle
6 radishes
2 avocados
lemon juice
Espelette pepper or smoked
   paprika, to taste
sea salt
150 g raisins
150 g walnuts, toasted
2 golden shallots, finely diced
⅓ cup white-wine vinegar
½ bunch lovage or celery,
   leaves picked

SOUR CUCUMBERS

1 teaspoon coriander seeds
1 teaspoon mustard seeds
1 teaspoon black peppercorns
1.5 litres water
½ bunch dill, leaves picked
1 bay leaf
6 cloves garlic, peeled
60 g sea salt
12 baby cucumbers, about
   8 cm long

PUFFED QUINOA

250 g white quinoa
grapeseed oil, to deep-fry
sea salt

Quinoa and avocado might be having a really trendy moment, but don't let this put you off! This is a healthy and nutritious salad that is wheat-free and high in calcium and magnesium. So while being tasty and versatile, it's pretty good for you too . . . and vegans love it!

To prepare the sour cucumbers, combine the seeds and peppercorns in a large saucepan. Cook over medium heat for a few minutes, shaking the pan occasionally, until brown and deeply aromatic. Remove from the heat.

Add the water to the pan, along with the dill, bay leaf, garlic and salt. Bring to the boil over medium–high heat, then transfer to a bowl and set aside to cool. Submerge the cucumbers in the cooled liquid. Use a heavy plate to keep them completely submerged. Leave at room temperature in a cool dark place for 1 week to sour.

For the puffed quinoa, preheat the oven to 60°C. Fill a large saucepan with water and bring to the boil over high heat. Add the white quinoa and cook at a rapid boil for 12–15 minutes, until tender. Don't worry about overcooking – the quinoa must be thoroughly cooked in order for it to puff correctly. Drain the quinoa and spread out on a tray. Dry overnight in a very low oven (30–40°C).

Half fill a medium saucepan with oil. Heat to 180°C. Working in 3–4 batches, place the cooked quinoa in a metal sieve and immerse in the oil. It should puff up very quickly, in about 1–2 seconds. If the oil is not hot enough it will not puff; if it is too hot it will quickly turn bitter. Transfer the puffed quinoa to a tray lined with paper towel and season with salt. Allow to cool.

Put the red quinoa in a fine sieve and rinse well under cold running water. Drain well. Place the quinoa in a large saucepan with the water, the juniper berries, bay leaf and salt. Cover and slowly bring to the boil over medium–low heat. Cook for 15–20 minutes or until the water has been absorbed by the quinoa. Discard the juniper berries and bay leaf and drizzle with oil.

Meanwhile, finely slice the radishes on a mandolin and submerge in a bowl of iced water to crisp them up. Remove the cucumbers from the brine, rinse thoroughly, and slice them on the mandolin to a similar thickness. Cut the avocados in half lengthways, remove the seeds and cut the flesh into long slices. Season the avocado with lemon juice, olive oil, Espelette pepper and salt.

Add the raisins, walnuts and shallot to the warm quinoa. Drizzle with the vinegar and season with salt. Transfer to a serving bowl and garnish with the avocado, radish, lovage or celery leaves and the puffed quinoa. Serve warm.

CHEF'S NOTE

A great gluten-free alternative in the modern world of allergies, protein- and fibre-rich quinoa offers a whole new world of interesting new salads and textures.

MARKET TIP

Quinoa comes in a number of colours, with red, white and black being the most common. They're all equally nutritious but be careful when cooking as they all differ slightly. Just choose the flavour and texture you like best.

Vine Tomatoes, Mozzarella, Olives

SERVES 8

100 g large green olives
½ cup pine nuts, toasted
2 tablespoons freshly
    chopped oregano
4 large mozzarella (about
    100 g each)
¼ cup extra virgin olive oil
1 lemon
1 bunch basil, leaves picked
sea salt
freshly ground black pepper

TOMATO CONFIT

1 kg roma tomatoes
⅓ cup extra virgin olive oil
2 teaspoons sugar
5 sprigs thyme
sea salt
freshly ground black pepper

MARINATED TOMATOES

1 kg mixed vine tomatoes,
    stems reserved (if present)
⅓ cup extra virgin olive oil
¼ cup aged balsamic vinegar
sea salt
freshly ground black pepper

This is a classic combination that really makes for a simple and tasty side dish in summer. Quick and easy, perfect for hot summer nights. You can use whatever varieties you can find for the marinated tomatoes, and a mixture is nice – the important thing is that they're perfectly ripe.

Preheat the oven to 80°C.

To make the tomato confit, bring a large pot of salted water to the boil, and prepare a large bowl of iced water. Using a paring knife, cut a small 'x' in the skin at the bottom of each tomato. Working in small batches, plunge the tomatoes into the boiling water for 15–30 seconds, until the skins begin to loosen. Remove with a slotted spoon and transfer to the iced water. Repeat with the remaining tomatoes.

Once the tomatoes are cool, drain well. Use a paring knife to peel off the skin – it should slide off fairly easily. Cut the tomatoes lengthways into quarters and remove the seeds. Place the tomato in a mixing bowl and add the olive oil, sugar and thyme. Season liberally with salt and pepper, and toss everything together.

Line a large baking tray with baking paper and lay the tomato out in a single layer. Place in the oven for 4–6 hours. They should be almost dry to the touch, but still moist on the palate. Discard the thyme. Cool the tomatoes and if not using straight away, cover and refrigerate. These can be made up to 2 days in advance.

For the marinated tomatoes, cut the larger tomatoes into quarters if you wish. Remove the cores, then slice into bite-sized wedges. Lay them seed-side up in a shallow glass or ceramic baking dish. Drizzle with olive oil and balsamic, and season liberally with salt and pepper. Refrigerate for 3–4 hours. Return to room temperature before serving.

To assemble, mix the olives, pine nuts, oregano, marinated tomatoes (and any liquid) and the tomato confit in a large bowl. Transfer to a large rimmed serving platter.

Gently tear the mozzarella into quarters and add to the tomatoes. Drizzle with olive oil. Grate the lemon zest finely over the mozzarella, then slice the lemon in half and squeeze the juice over the cheese.

Decorate the salad with the basil leaves, season with salt and pepper, and serve.

CHEF'S NOTE

Such simple dishes rely on the quality of the ingredients, but most importantly the balance is paramount. That means the seasoning must be perfect: I like to add a pinch of sugar to cut through the tart, sharp flavour of the tomatoes and also a few good twists of freshly ground pepper.

MARKET TIP

Use great local olive oil for this dressing and make sure you have the balance of sweet, sour and fresh pepper just right. As a general rule, ⅔ oil to ⅓ vinegar is perfect for most vinaigrettes.

Charred Cos, Caper, Anchovy, Chives

SERVES 4

2 heads baby cos lettuce
3 tablespoons capers in brine,
    rinsed and drained
grapeseed oil, to deep-fry
sea salt, to season
anchovies, to serve

CREME FRAICHE DRESSING
300 g crème fraîche
½ bunch chives, finely
    chopped
3 anchovies
30 ml olive oil
juice of 2 limes
sea salt
freshly ground black pepper

Sometimes simple salads are the best. This one has smoky notes from charring the lettuce, acid from the capers, and salty fishy flavours from the anchovy with a hint of delicate onion from the chives.

Fill a large bowl with cold water. Trim the bottom of the lettuce stems and remove any damaged outer leaves to reveal a crisp, bright core. Cut lengthways into quarters and submerge in the water for a few minutes. Remove from the water and place cut-side down on a clean tea towel to dry for at least 1 hour.

Meanwhile, drain the capers and lay out on paper towel for a few minutes to dry. Pour enough oil into a medium saucepan so it is just under half full. Heat over medium heat to 160°C. Place the capers into a small metal sieve and immerse in the oil. Fry for 1–2 minutes, until crisp. Transfer to a plate lined with paper towel to drain and cool.

To make the dressing, combine the crème fraîche and chives in a mixing bowl. On a cutting board, use a fork or the flat side of a knife to crush the anchovies to a paste, then add to the crème fraîche mixture. Stir in the olive oil and lime juice. Season with salt and pepper.

Preheat a barbecue grillplate on high heat. Once the grill is very hot, grease it with oil. Lightly salt the lettuce quarters and place cut-side down on the grill. Cook for about 2–3 minutes, until they have deep, dark grill lines. Turn the lettuce to the other cut side and cook for the same time.

Remove the lettuce from the grill and arrange on a serving platter. Smear the dressing along the cooked sides – you almost cannot use too much. Garnish simply with anchovies and fried capers.

CHEF'S NOTE

If you don't have time or are not a fan of grilling and charring lettuce, this salad works well with fresh cos or even iceberg lettuce – an old favourite, but nothing beats that crunch!

MARKET TIP

There are lots of different anchovies on the market, but you get what you pay for, as with everything in life! Always buy a high-quality anchovy that has a delicate, salty seafood flavour and is not too 'fishy'. I like to use Ortiz anchovies (and their sardines are wonderful, too).

Kipfler Potatoes,
Sour Cream, Saltbush

Salty . Texture . Sour

SERVES 8–10

2 sprigs saltbush leaves
grapeseed oil, to deep-fry
1 kg baby kipfler
    potatoes, scrubbed
sea salt
3 bay leaves
5 sprigs thyme
2 golden shallots,
    finely chopped
150 ml extra virgin olive oil
¼ cup champagne vinegar
freshly ground black pepper

SOUR CREAM DRESSING

250 g sour cream
45 ml lemon juice
1 bunch dill, leaves
    finely chopped
1 red onion, finely diced
sea salt
freshly ground black pepper

What is this dish? A potato salad? A rough 'mash'? This dish is almost an *écrasse*, which in French means 'crushed'. It's really just a rustic potato dish that soaks up all the lovely juices of the vinaigrette and the sour cream! The addition of some crispy saltbush really adds another dimension. A little tip: buying potatoes from a local grower or farmers' market really makes a massive difference. Fresh from the ground gives an exceptional flavour and texture.

For the dressing, combine the sour cream, juice, dill and onion in a bowl and season with salt and pepper to taste. Cover and refrigerate until needed.

Gently wash the saltbush leaves. Drain and dry in a salad spinner. Pour enough oil into a medium saucepan so it is just under half full. Heat over medium-high heat to 180°C. Working in batches, place the saltbush leaves into a metal sieve and immerse in the oil – they will spit a lot at first due to the water content. Fry for about 30 seconds, but don't let them colour at all. Transfer to a plate lined with paper towel to drain and cool.

Place the potatoes into a large saucepan of cold salted water with the bay leaves and thyme. Slowly bring the water to a simmer over medium-low heat then cook for 8–10 minutes, or until the potatoes are tender when pierced with a knife.

Meanwhile, combine the shallot, olive oil and vinegar in a small saucepan. Season generously with pepper. Place over low heat and gently simmer for 2–3 minutes, until the shallot is translucent and the pepper flavour has infused the dressing.

Drain the potatoes and place in a large mixing bowl. Gently break each potato into 2–3 pieces, exposing the fluffy, steaming hot interior. Pour the warm shallot mixture over the potatoes and gently toss to coat, taking care not to break the potatoes too much more or turn them into a mash. Drizzle with a little more olive oil if too dry. Transfer to a serving bowl and garnish with fried saltbush. Serve with the sour cream dressing on the side.

CHEF'S NOTE

If you can't find kipfler potatoes, have a look around for any baby new season's potatoes. My favourite for salads are bontje, desiree or pink eye. Sebago or nicola are other good all rounders.

MARKET TIP

Don't go to the market! Saltbush grows wild all along the coast of Victoria and is a wonderful, hearty leaf. Once fried it adds a wonderful crisp texture and a natural salinity to anything you garnish with it. If you can't get it, you can fry sage leaves instead.

Shaved Zucchini, Prosciutto, Goat's Curd

SERVES 6

3 medium green zucchini
3 medium yellow squash
300 g thinly sliced prosciutto
200 g goat's curd
100 g macadamias, toasted
    and roughly chopped
¼ bunch basil, leaves picked
¼ bunch flat-leaf parsley,
    leaves picked
¼ bunch tarragon,
    leaves picked

GOAT'S CURD MERINGUE
250 g goat's curd
2 egg whites
finely grated zest of 2 lemons
sea salt, to season

TARRAGON VINAIGRETTE
200 ml grapeseed oil
100 g tarragon leaves
50 g flat-leaf parsley leaves
100 ml lemon juice

Most people like to grill or sauté their zucchini, but shaved raw is equally as delicious, and it also has a wonderful crisp texture. The goat's cheese meringue, while sounding complex, is pretty straightforward and a great little 'wow' moment as it brings a new texture into the dish.

To make the meringue, preheat the oven to 60°C fan-forced. Using a spatula, combine the goat's curd, egg white and lemon zest in a mixing bowl and season with sea salt. There is no need to whip the whites.

Line a baking tray with baking paper. Using an offset pallet knife, spread the mixture evenly across the paper to about 3 mm thickness.

Place the tray in the oven and leave overnight to dry. The result should be a flat, crispy meringue. Break into chips about 3 cm wide and store in an airtight container at room temperature until ready to use. It will keep for 1–2 days.

For the vinaigrette, place the oil in a blender and turn on low speed. With the motor running, drop the leaves into the oil through the hole in the lid a few at a time. When all the leaves have been added, turn the mixer up to high speed and blend for 1–2 minutes, until the oil is steaming. Transfer to a mixing bowl and stand in a larger bowl of ice. Cool quickly, stirring to release the heat. Cover and refrigerate overnight.

In the morning, place a sieve across a mixing bowl and line the sieve with a coffee filter. Pour the oil through the coffee filter and leave for a few hours for it to drip through. Complete the dressing by combining the herb oil and the juice just before assembling the salad.

To assemble the salad, use a mandolin to shave the zucchini and squash lengthways into strips about 1.5 mm thick. Lay out on a flat surface and season lightly with salt.

Roll and fold the zucchini and squash on a serving platter. Do the same with the prosciutto, interleaving it with the zucchini. Dollop the goat's curd evenly throughout the platter, sprinkle with macadamias and garnish with the herb leaves. Drizzle with tarragon dressing and finish with the goat's curd meringue.

CHEF'S NOTE

For something different you can always crisp or cook your prosciutto quickly under the grill. It adds great texture and is a bit like a glamorous crispy bacon. The tarragon oil can hold for a day or two but shouldn't be combined with the lemon juice until nearly ready to serve as the acid will destroy the chlorophyll, which gives the oil its vibrant colour.

MARKET TIP

It's easy to be scared of goat's cheese, but don't be! There are a lot of different types around, so just find one that suits your palate. And if you really can't stomach it, then look at other soft cheeses or curds.

Peach and Marzipan Cream,
Barbecued Peaches

Temperature . Texture . Sweet

SERVES 4–6

**PEACH AND
MARZIPAN CREAM**
200 g peach puree
200 g marzipan, chopped
400 ml whipping cream
pinch of sea salt

BARBECUED PEACHES
3 large ripe yellow peaches
1 tablespoon vegetable oil
2 tablespoons honey, plus
    extra to serve (optional)
butter (optional)

ALMOND FLAKES
125 g flaked almonds
1 egg white, lightly whisked
40 g caster sugar

Marzipan might sound fancy but it's really just an almond paste made with sugar or honey. It's delicious when added to a bit of cream. If you have access to direct fire or coals, then cooking on those really does take the barbecued peaches to the next level.

To make the peach and marzipan cream, combine the peach purée and marzipan in a blender and blend on high until smooth. Transfer to a mixing bowl. Whip the cream to firm peaks. Gently fold the whipped cream into the marzipan mixture in 3 batches. Season with salt and store in piping bags or plastic storage containers in the fridge.

To make the barbecued peaches, halve each fruit lengthways and remove the stones. Preheat a grillplate or barbecue to high. Oil the cut-side of the peaches slightly to ensure they do not stick to the grill.

Place the peaches cut-side down on the grill and cook for 3–4 minutes before turning over to the other side for 2–3 minutes. Just before you take the peaches off drizzle them with honey and turn them over to caramelise lightly. Do not burn. You can also choose to add a small knob of butter as well. Remove from the grill and set aside.

For the almond flakes, preheat the oven to 165°C and line a baking tray with baking paper. Coat the almonds well with the egg white, followed by the sugar. Spread on the prepared tray and bake for 6 minutes then turn the tray around and bake for another 4–6 minutes, or until golden and caramelised. Leave to cool.

To serve, pipe or spoon a generous amount of the peach and marzipan cream onto each serving plate. Add a peach half, drizzle with extra honey (if using) and sprinkle with almond flakes.

CHEF'S NOTE
If you don't have access to a barbecue or grillplate, then roasting the peaches in the oven with a bit of caramel also gives you great results. If you like, finish this dish with a good drizzle of a Tasmanian leatherwood honey, as it adds a lovely floral, earthy note.

TO DRINK
Here I would choose a dense and aromatic wine from the pinot gris varietal. When it's late-harvest the pinot gris shows spices, dry grape and honey notes. Originally from Alsace in the east of France, great examples are also produced here in Australia.

MARKET TIP
I use peaches in this recipe, but other stone fruits such as nectarines or plums grill really well too. You can make the peach purée by blending the flesh of ripe peaches, or buy it frozen or tinned.

Toasted Barley Crème Brûlée, Peppered Strawberries

Spicy . Sweet . Texture

SERVES 6

CREME BRULEE
50 g pearl barley
350 g cream
250 g milk
150 g caster sugar
12 egg yolks
½ teaspoon salt
¼ cup demerara
   or brown sugar

PUFFED PEARL BARLEY
100 g pearl barley
grapeseed oil, to deep-fry
sea salt, to season

PEPPERED STRAWBERRIES
½ teaspoon black
   peppercorns
½ teaspoon pink peppercorns
½ teaspoon
   sichuan peppercorns
1 star anise
5 cloves
100 g demerara sugar
250 g strawberries, washed
   and hulled
8 basil leaves, finely shredded

The toasty notes of puffed barley in this recipe provide an interesting take on an otherwise classic crème brûlée. The peppered strawberries give extra punch and are mellowed out by the crème.

To make the crème brûlée, preheat the oven to 180°C. Spread the barley in a single layer on a baking tray and bake for 15–20 minutes, until toasted. Meanwhile, combine the cream and milk in a bowl. Add the hot toasted barley. Cover and leave to infuse in the fridge overnight.

The next day, preheat the oven to 150°C. Strain the barley from the milk and cream. You should be left with 400 ml liquid. Place the liquid in a saucepan over medium heat. Bring to a simmer, then remove from the heat.

Whisk the sugar and egg yolks in a bowl until pale and creamy. Pour one-third of the warm milk mixture onto the whisked yolks, stirring to combine. Pour back into the remaining milk mixture. Whisk in salt and strain into a jug.

Line the base of a roasting pan with a folded tea towel. Place six 250 ml capacity ceramic dishes on the tea towel and pour the mixture into them. Cover the pan with foil, leaving one corner open. Place the pan in the oven and pour in enough boiling water (through the open corner) to come halfway up the sides of the dishes. Close the foil and bake for 50–55 minutes or until the custards are just slightly wobbly in the centre. Lift dishes out of the water and leave to cool for 15 minutes. Transfer to the fridge to set overnight.

To make the puffed pearl barley, bring a large saucepan of water to the boil and add the barley. Reduce to a simmer, and cook for about 1 hour until very tender.

Preheat the oven to 75°C and line a large baking tray with baking paper. Drain the barley through a sieve and rinse under cold running water. Spread out on the prepared baking tray in a single layer. Place in the oven for about 3–4 hours, until dry.

Pour enough oil into a medium saucepan so it is half full. Heat over medium–high heat to 180°C. Working in batches, place a small handful of barley into a metal sieve and fry for about 30 seconds until puffed. Drain on a tray lined with paper towel and season with a small amount of salt.

For the peppered strawberries, combine the spices in a frying pan and cook for a few minutes over medium heat, shaking the pan occasionally, until fragrant and lightly toasted. Transfer to a plate to cool. Blitz the cooled spices in a spice grinder or small food processor. Add the sugar and blitz again to a fine dust.

Slice the strawberries into rounds and season liberally with the peppered sugar and basil. Leave to macerate in a bowl for about 4 minutes before serving. Keep any leftover sugar in an airtight container for up to 4 weeks.

Sprinkle each custard with 2 teaspoons demerara or brown sugar. Use a kitchen blow torch to caramelise the sugar to a dark amber. Leave to cool for 1 minute.

To serve, spoon the strawberries and basil and some puffed barley onto each brulee.

CHEF'S NOTE

I love to take a classic dish and mix it up a bit. A dairy-based dessert like this one is such a wonderful vehicle for different flavour combinations. You could do things like lemon verbena, lavender or even thyme. The options are endless.

TO DRINK

To marry the berries and spice, a low-sugar rosé is perfect. The crunchiness of the barley and the sugar crust call for some fizz. A great example of this wine is produced on the eastern side of France in the Bugey region: hunt for a cerdon.

MARKET TIP

Taste, taste, taste. Something like a strawberry can look wonderful but have no real flavour. Choose big, juicy ripe ones and I sometimes even have a cheeky taste when I'm buying them just to make sure they are delicious!

Poached Cherries, Burnt White Chocolate, Crème Fraîche Sorbet

Temperature . Bitter . Sweet

SERVES 8

CREME FRAICHE SORBET

110 g caster sugar
35 g liquid glucose
100 ml water
260 ml cream
260 g crème fraîche
juice of ½ lemon

CANDIED PISTACHIOS

30 g sugar
1 tablespoon honey
½ teaspoon water
4 tablespoons unsalted
  pistachios
pinch of salt

POACHED CHERRIES

80 ml kirsch
175 g caster sugar
1 vanilla bean, split,
  seeds scraped
strips of zest and juice
  of 1 lemon
½ cinnamon stick
2 star anise
600 ml water
750 g cherries, pitted
  and halved

BURNT WHITE CHOCOLATE CREAM

540 ml cream
215 ml milk
100 g caster sugar
10 egg yolks
½ teaspoon salt
175 g white chocolate, melted
  and cooled

When designing dishes, we always look for different elements to excite the tastebuds. The burnt white chocolate cream here is an example of that, bringing out the nutty notes of the cocoa bean and adding a different dimension to the dish. The crème fraîche sorbet is refreshing and cuts through the fat content of the chocolate, while the pistachio adds a nutty flavour to complement the poached fruit.

To make the sorbet, combine the sugar, glucose and water in a saucepan over medium heat. Stir to dissolve the sugar, then bring to the boil. Remove from the heat and whisk in the cream, then the crème fraîche and lemon juice. Pass through a fine sieve into a bowl over ice, stirring to release the heat. Once cooled, churn in an ice-cream machine. Transfer to an airtight container and freeze.

To make the candied pistachios, line a baking tray with baking paper. Combine the sugar, honey and water in a saucepan. Dissolve the sugar over medium heat until a syrup forms. Add the pistachios and salt and cook for 2 minutes over medium heat. Remove from the heat and spread the mixture over the prepared tray to allow it to cool down. Once cool, crush with a rolling pin in order to create crumbs of candied pistachio.

For the poached cherries, combine the kirsch, sugar, vanilla bean and seeds, lemon zest, cinnamon stick, star anise and water in a saucepan over medium heat. Stir until sugar dissolves, then bring to the boil. Add the cherries and lemon juice. Cover the fruit with a round of baking paper, ensuring the fruit is submerged in the syrup. Reduce to low heat and cook for 8 minutes. Allow the fruit to cool in the syrup until it reaches room temperature. Transfer to a storage container with enough syrup to cover the fruit and refrigerate. Strain and reduce leftover syrup to a sticky glaze.

To make the burnt white chocolate cream, preheat the oven to 175°C. Combine the cream and milk in a saucepan and bring to a simmer. Whisk the sugar and egg yolks in a mixing bowl until pale and creamy. Pour the hot milk and cream mixture over the yolk mixture, stirring to combine. Pass through a fine sieve into a deep tray (25 cm × 15 cm) and bake for 40 minutes or until the top is golden and caramelised. Set aside for 25 minutes to cool. Once cooled, transfer the cream to a blender and blitz with the white chocolate 45–60 seconds on high. Pass through a sieve into a bowl sitting in a larger bowl of ice. Leave to cool.

To serve, drain the cherries on paper towel. Spoon a generous mound of the burnt white chocolate cream into the centre of each serving plate. Use a hot spoon make a dip in the middle of the mound. Dress the cherries with the reduced syrup and place into the dip. Use a warm spoon to scoop some of the crème fraîche sorbet on the side and sprinkle with the candied pistachios.

CHEF'S NOTE

Get some other guy to pip the cherries!

TO DRINK

A fortified wine will have the structure to shine with the cold sorbet and the sweetness of the cream. Here I choose a rosé and I'd serve it at 10–12 degrees. You can find many good options from the Douro Valley in Portugal.

MARKET TIP

There are varying grades of cherries, and for poaching they don't necessarily have to be A grade. The ripe and juicy ones are normally better for poaching, while the premium ones can be reserved for table displays and eating on their own.

Fromage Blanc Panna Cotta, Summer Berries, Crispy Almond Filo

SERVES 6

125 g blueberries
125 g raspberries
250 g strawberries, hulled
  and sliced

PANNA COTTA
2 × 2.2 g gelatine leaves
  (gold strength)
220 ml cream
100 g caster sugar
30 lemon verbena leaves
  or zest from 2 lemons
  and 2 limes
1 vanilla bean, split,
  seeds scraped
450 g fromage blanc
neutral oil, such as grapeseed
  oil, for greasing (optional)

CRISPY ALMOND FILO
80 g butter
⅓ cup honey
6 sheets filo pastry
50 g ground almonds

The literal translation of fromage blanc is 'white cheese'. It's a soft and creamy cheese that is similar to cream cheese but with less fat, making it perfect to spruce up your panna cotta (which in Italian means 'cooked cream'). You can find it in cheese shops or at good markets like the Queen Vic in Melbourne, or a good substitute is Greek-style yoghurt.

To make the panna cotta, place the gelatine leaves in a bowl of iced water for 5 minutes, to soften. Combine the cream, sugar, verbena and vanilla bean and seeds in a small saucepan and bring to the boil. Remove from the heat. Squeeze excess water from the gelatine and add to the hot cream mixture. Stir to dissolve, then set aside to cool for 5 minutes.

Put the fromage blanc in a mixing bowl and strain the cream mixture over. Blend with a stick blender until smooth and evenly combined.

Choose six pretty serving glasses or lightly oil six 200 ml capacity moulds if you want to turn the panna cotta out later. Strain the fromage blanc mixture into a jug and pour into the glasses or moulds. Alternatively, pour the mixture into a bowl to be scooped out to serve. Place in the fridge to set for at least 6 hours, or preferably overnight.

For the crispy almond filo, preheat the oven to 180°C. Line 2 large heavy baking trays with baking paper, and have 2 more sheets of baking paper and 2 more large heavy baking trays ready.

Gently melt the butter and honey together in a small saucepan until combined. Remove from the heat. Lay the filo out on the work bench and cover with a damp tea towel to prevent it drying out while you work.

Put one sheet of filo on a baking tray and brush with the butter mixture, coating the whole surface. Sprinkle with ground almonds. Lay another filo sheet on top, brush with butter mixture and sprinkle with ground almonds. Top with another filo sheet. Repeat on another baking tray to make another stack of 3 filo sheets.

Top each stack with a sheet of baking paper and a baking tray to help keep the filo flat. Bake for 10–15 minutes or until golden and crispy. Transfer to a wire rack to cool, then break into desired shapes.

Depending on how you have set the panna cotta, serve it in the glass, turn it out or spoon it onto a plate. Garnish with berries and serve with filo shards.

CHEF'S NOTE

Be careful if removing the panna cotta from moulds: it's a delicate dessert and we always try to take it right to the edge in terms of being as 'just set' as possible. If you don't have any moulds, pour the mixture into a bowl and spoon the panna cotta directly onto serving plates.

TO DRINK

A prosecco frizzante: the small, light bubbles will brighten up the texture of the panna cotta, while the sweet and citrusy flavour will echo the lemon verbena aromas from the cream. What's more, the acidity from the wine will match the acidity of berries to make a perfect pairing.

MARKET TIP

Don't feel like you have to be restricted to just serving this panna cotta with summer berries. You can use grilled peaches, poached cherries or even fresh figs in summer.

Grilled Figs, Cinnamon Ricotta Dumplings, Orange

SERVES 6

CANDIED ORANGE ZEST
4 oranges
150 g caster sugar
75 g liquid glucose
225 g caster sugar, extra
150 ml water

WHIPPED MASCARPONE
250 g mascarpone
25 g icing sugar, sifted
finely grated zest and juice
   of 1 orange

**CINNAMON RICOTTA
DUMPLINGS**
grapeseed oil, to deep-fry
80 g plain flour
40 g caster sugar
½ teaspoon ground cinnamon
¼ teaspoon baking powder
finely grated zest of 2 oranges
2 eggs
1 egg yolk
500 g ricotta
caster sugar, to dust

GRILLED FIGS
6 figs, halved lengthways
honey, to drizzle

I've given this one a little Italian slant by adding ricotta dumplings and mascarpone to the mix. Full of flavour and texture, this really is a decadent dessert.

To make the candied orange zest, peel the skin from the oranges in wide strips. Use a small sharp knife to remove the white pith, then cut the peel into fine strips. Place in a small saucepan of cold water with 2 tablespoons of the sugar and bring to the boil. Once brought to a boil strain and refresh in iced water. Repeat the process 4 times, with fresh water and another 2 tablespoons of sugar each time.

In another saucepan, combine the glucose, extra sugar and the water, and stir over medium heat until the sugar has dissolved. Bring to the boil and cook until the mixture reaches 108°C on a sugar thermometer. Remove from the heat, add the blanched orange zest and set aside to cool completely. Lift the zest from the syrup and drain on a wire rack.

For the whipped mascarpone, use an electric stand mixer to beat the mascarpone, icing sugar, orange zest and juice for 20–30 seconds, just to very soft peaks. Do not overbeat or it may split. Store in an airtight container in the fridge until needed.

To make the cinnamon ricotta dumplings, pour enough oil into a large saucepan so it is just under half full. Heat to 180°C. Mix the flour, sugar, cinnamon, baking powder, orange zest, eggs and yolk to a smooth paste. Slowly mix in the ricotta until incorporated.

Transfer the mixture to a piping bag fitted with a plain 3 cm nozzle. Working in batches so you don't overcrowd the pan, pipe 5–6 cm lengths of mixture straight into the hot oil, snipping it off with kitchen scissors. Deep-fry for 2–3 minutes, keeping the dumplings moving in the oil to brown evenly. Alternatively, you can quenelle the mixture with 2 teaspoons. If so, cook for a few moments longer as they will be larger. Drain on a tray lined with paper towel and dust with a light sprinkle of caster sugar as they cool.

For the grilled figs, arrange the figs cut-side up on a baking tray and drizzle with honey. Cook under a hot grill until caramelised.

To serve, place 2 warm fig halves on each serving plate and add ricotta dumplings. Add a spoonful of the whipped mascarpone and finish with a few strands of the candied zest.

CHEF'S NOTE

We had two fig trees in our backyard for years and years until they finally had to make way for a new yard for the kids, and I still miss them. The problem was the birds used to eat almost as many as me! We had black and green figs, which would ripen at different times . . . ah, my old fig trees.

TO DRINK

You need a complex wine able to match the different flavours from the food and I'd recommend one of the most renowned dessert wines in the world: the Hungarian tokaji aszu. Select it with 3 or 4 puttonyos (level of sweetness), very concentrated – above this level of sugar the match might be too rich.

MARKET TIP

Figs: such a versatile fruit, they're great for jams, chutneys, fruit salads or even just to snack on. They let me know that summer has well and truly arrived. Try and choose nice soft figs that feel 'heavy' and look like they are about to burst.

Tomatoes.

Once tomatoes have arrived, I really know that summer is coming. Sliced simply and dressed with a great extra virgin olive oil, sea salt and pepper, some torn fresh basil … I'm in heaven. You could also pair them with olives (both green and black), pickled shallots, leftover bread for some crunch, or sliced on some buttery toast with a tasty soft cheese such as ricotta or goat's cheese. And tomatoes are perfect for a hot or cold soup, a purée or sauce base, some fresh handmade pasta or even dried and preserved for later in the year. Sometimes the basics really are my favourites.

Strawberries.

The humble strawberry is a winner with so many things: cultured cream, custard, meringue … Serve them raw, poached, baked, roasted, in a pudding, a soufflé, a tart or an ice-cream – endless options. There is even a crossover between these two heroes: tomatoes work well with green strawberries, as does basil, thanks to the herbaceous notes that create a lovely balance between sweet and savoury. Experiment and enjoy the results.

Summer Menu I

STARTER

Hiramasa Kingfish, Finger Lime, White Soy

(page 64)

MAIN

Whole Flounder Grenobloise

(page 79)

SIDES

Vine Tomatoes, Mozzarella, Olives

(page 82)

Charred Cos, Caper, Anchovy, Chives

(page 84)

DESSERT

Fromage Blanc Panna Cotta, Summer Berries, Crispy Almond Filo

(page 97)

Summer Menu 2

STARTER

Grilled Calamari, Preserved Lemon Gremolata

(page 66)

MAIN

Slow-roasted Pork Shoulder, Lemon Thyme, Garlic

(page 80)

SIDES

Kipfler Potatoes, Sour Cream, Saltbush

(page 87)

Shaved Zucchini, Prosciutto, Goat's Curd

(page 88)

DESSERT

Peach and Marzipan Cream, Barbecued Peaches

(page 90)

Autumn

When the days start to get cooler, and the long, hot summer nights start to disappear, you know that autumn is just around the corner. The cooler, moist mornings are the perfect environment for the growth of wild mushrooms: pines, slippery jacks, grey ghosts and morels. Quinces become fragrant and ripe, ready for slow poaching and jams and preserves. One of the best but most under-used root vegetables, Jerusalem artichokes are perfect for a soup, roasted or fried.

What I find most interesting about the change of the seasons is that, for me, they are based around colour. For as long as I can remember, I've been intrigued by the emotion that comes with each season and the link between the climate, the temperature, my surroundings, the colours of the trees and their leaves . . . the change in my mood, that spark in my soul when summer arrives, or the little boy inside me who wants to crawl under the covers and go back to sleep when it's dark and wet outside. The impact that this has on what we choose to eat at different times of year, and how that food makes us feel, still fascinates me no end.

Whereas summer is bright with its splashes of red, orange and yellow, winter is deep and dark. And, of course, spring must most certainly be green, my mood blossoming like the early signs of reborn plant life all around me. On the other hand, autumn's fruits and wares evoke shades of tan, soft browns and earthy, natural tones. It's a time of rich flavours and reflection.

Salt-baked Beetroot, Macadamia, Purslane

SERVES 6

1 bunch golden baby beetroot,
    finely shaved
1 bunch candy baby beetroot,
    finely shaved
extra virgin olive oil, to dress
sea salt
1 bunch purslane
    or rocket, washed

MACADAMIA PUREE

250 g macadamias
1 bunch thyme, leaves picked
olive oil, to drizzle
sea salt

SALT-BAKED BEETROOT

1 kg plain flour
500 g fine cooking salt
300 ml water
6 large beetroot (about 200 g
    each), washed and dried

BEETROOT DRESSING

4 beetroot, washed
50 ml balsamic vinegar
50 ml olive oil
sea salt

Salt baking is an interesting and different technique that really captures the true essence of the ingredient. Adding a native nut like macadamia gives this a true Aussie feeling, and an interesting herb like succulent, herbaceous purslane separates you from the pack!

To make the macadamia purée, preheat the oven to 180°C. Combine the macadamias and thyme in a bowl. Drizzle lightly with oil, season with salt and toss to coat. Place on a baking tray and cook for 6–8 minutes, until golden. Set aside to cool. Keep about 10 roasted macadamias for serving and place the rest in a food processor. Process until smooth. Refrigerate the purée until required (it will keep for up to 3 days), but return to room temperature to serve.

For the salt-baked beetroot, combine the flour and salt in a large mixing bowl and make a well in the centre. Gradually add the water and mix to a dough. Gather together and knead until smooth. Roll the dough out to 2 cm thickness and place on a large baking tray. Sit the beetroot on the dough, evenly spaced, and cut the dough between them so each beetroot is sitting on its own individual rough circle of dough. Fold the dough over to enclose each one, pressing to seal. Bake for 1 hour, then set aside to cool to room temperature. Carefully break the dough and prise out the beetroot. Cut each beetroot into 6 wedges.

To make the beetroot dressing, juice the 4 beetroot and measure 200 ml juice. Place in a small saucepan over low heat, and simmer until reduced to 75 ml. Cool. Combine the beetroot reduction with the balsamic vinegar and olive oil. Season with salt.

Dress the shaved baby beetroot with olive oil and salt and set aside. Shave the reserved macadamias. To assemble, spread a thin layer of macadamia purée on the base of each plate. Season the warm beetroot wedges with salt and arrange on top of the purée. Delicately place the purslane over and around the beetroot. Spoon the dressing over, and add the shaved beetroot and macadamias. Drizzle with a little olive oil, and serve.

CHEF'S NOTE

Don't limit yourself to just salt-baking beetroot – this method works really well with celeriac, turnips, and even pumpkin. It can also be used to add flavour to large cuts of beef, like a rib eye, keeping them moist and juicy.

TO DRINK

The sweetness of the beetroot and freshness of purslane give us a great occasion to serve a simple juicy red at cellar temperature. Maybe an opportunity to try a natural wine producer. Choose a fruit-forward red with low tannins.

MARKET TIP

Use different types of heirloom and heritage beetroot to garnish this warm salad. Yellow, target, pink and white beetroot add some wonderful colour to a really tasty combination.

Gold Band Snapper, Shiitake, Brown Butter

SERVES 4

4 x 250 g fillets gold
   band snapper
sea salt
drizzle of olive oil
100 g butter
500 g shiitake
   mushrooms, sliced
100 ml lemon juice
freshly ground black pepper
50 g flat-leaf parsley, leaves
   finely chopped

Mushrooms and brown butter. Not too much else to say, really, as this is a perfect combination: fat, umami, salt and wonderful autumnal tones . . . Just don't forget a good squeeze of acid to cut through the rich fat.

Score the skin on the fish fillets, without cutting into the flesh. Season both sides with salt. Preheat a heavy-based or cast-iron frying pan over medium heat. Add the oil to the pan and cook the fish skin-side up for 3 minutes, then turn and cook for 1 minute with the skin-side down. Transfer to a tray lined with paper towel to absorb excess oil.

Wipe out the pan. Add the butter and when it begins to foam and turn brown, add the mushrooms and sauté until soft. Season with the lemon juice, salt and pepper and stir in the parsley.

Spoon the mushroom mixture and the buttery juices onto serving plates. Top with the fish, skin-side up, and serve.

CHEF'S NOTE

Beurre noisette or brown butter is a quick and tasty base for sauces, dressing and vinaigrettes. Either made beforehand or *à la minute*, make sure you cook your butter to that wonderful nutty stage – but be careful, not too far or else it will burn!

TO DRINK

The umami flavour from the shiitake alongside the purity of the snapper's flesh provides the perfect opportunity to get familiar with Georgian wine. The particularity of this old traditional wine country is to produce wine in amphora resulting in an incredible purity. I would drink an orange wine as an unusual pick. You will have a great talking point at the table!

MARKET TIP

I've used shiitake mushrooms in this recipe because they are pretty easy to find these days, but if you're at the markets and see some wonderful wild ones, they can be a great substitute. Think pine mushrooms, slippery jacks or on the rare occasion here in Oz you might be lucky enough to find a local morel!

Octopus, Skordalia, Oregano

SERVES 8–10

OCTOPUS
1 × 700 g whole
    octopus, cleaned
2 litres canola oil
100 g golden shallots, sliced
1 teaspoon black peppercorns
1 bunch thyme
2 bulbs garlic, bashed
peel of 1 lemon, cut into
    wide strips

OREGANO DRESSING
½ bunch oregano, leaves picked
100 ml olive oil
50 ml white balsamic vinegar
sea salt
freshly ground black pepper

SKORDALIA
1 kg desiree potatoes, peeled
    and chopped
100 ml olive oil
6 cloves garlic, chopped
1 tablespoon lemon juice
sea salt
¾ cup chopped flat-leaf
    parsley (optional)

The Greeks probably cook octopus better than anyone, so I've used their heritage and experience to adapt a centuries-old flavour combination using a French braising technique. Skordalia is versatile too, and is delicious used as a spread or dip.

To prepare the octopus, wash well then place in a large bowl and knead 40 times (like a massage!). When the octopus tentacles begin to curl, then you know it is ready to cook.

Combine the canola oil, shallot, peppercorns, thyme, garlic and lemon peel in a large pot. Heat to 90°C. Add the octopus and cook gently over low heat for 1 hour. Take off the heat and allow the octopus to cool to room temperature in the oil. Remove the octopus from the pot.

To make the oregano dressing, combine all the ingredients in a bowl and season well with salt and pepper.

For the skordalia, cook the potatoes in a large saucepan of salted boiling water until tender. Drain, then let the steam evaporate off. Heat the olive oil in a saucepan over low heat and simmer the garlic for 2 minutes, without browning. Add the soft potato and whisk to a smooth purée. Season with lemon juice and salt, and stir in parsley if using.

To serve, season the octopus with the oregano dressing. Spoon the skordalia onto a serving plate and arrange the octopus on top, finishing with a squeeze of lemon if you wish.

CHEF'S NOTE

Wash your octopus thoroughly before cooking. The octopus will keep in the fridge, covered in the marinade, for a couple of weeks. That way it's always on hand for a light snack, a charcuterie board or as a tasty lunch on some fresh baguette.

TO DRINK

A very popular dish in Santorini. There, a classic pairing with octopus is the assyrtiko, traditionally grown on the island. Alternatively, a fiano would provide texture and intensity to stand in front of the garlic of the skordalia. Originally from southern Italy and Sicily, you can find amazing examples of fiano from Victoria and South Australia and also Argentina.

MARKET TIP

If you don't like cooking large octopus, you can quite often find little baby octopus at the markets these days too. You can use this same recipe and cooking technique, just adjust the cooking time. I'd say check them after 30–40 minutes and they should be ready.

Gnocchi, Gorgonzola, Silverbeet

SERVES 8

GNOCCHI
500 g rock salt
1 kg sebago potatoes,
    (or similar), scrubbed
220 g '00' flour
75 g parmesan, finely grated
1 tablespoon olive oil
1 egg
1 egg yolk
pinch of ground nutmeg
pinch of sea salt

**GORGONZOLA AND
SILVERBEET CREAM**
150 ml white wine
2 golden shallots, peeled
    and sliced
1 bay leaf
6 black peppercorns
250 ml chicken stock
    (or vegetable if you prefer)
500 ml cream
150 g good-quality
    gorgonzola, crumbled
½ lemon
50 ml olive oil
sea salt
freshly ground black pepper
1 bunch silverbeet, washed
    and dried

I'm a big lover of blue cheese, and fat. So when it's in a cream-based sauce, with wonderful, light pillows of potato gnocchi, I'm pretty much in heaven! Silverbeet is a bit of a 'poor man's vegetable' but adds another dimension to this classic dish.
It serves 8 as a starter, but you could also enjoy it as a main dish for 4 people.

For the gnocchi, preheat the oven to 180°C. Spread the rock salt thickly onto a baking tray and sit the potatoes on it. Bake for 1–1½ hours, until very tender when pierced with a knife.

Cut potatoes in half lengthways, scoop out the flesh and pass through a mouli or potato ricer into a large mixing bowl. While still warm add the flour, parmesan, olive oil, egg and egg yolk. Season with nutmeg and salt. Gently mix together, then gather the dough and turn out onto a lightly floured bench.

Divide the dough into 4 portions. Roll into logs 2 cm wide and cut each log into 2 cm pieces. Bring a large pot of salted water to the boil.

Meanwhile, to make the gorgonzola and silverbeet cream, combine the wine, shallot, bay leaf and peppercorns in a small saucepan over medium heat. Bring to the boil and cook until reduced by two-thirds. Add the stock and boil until again reduced by two-thirds. Stir in the cream and cook until reduced by half. Pass through a fine sieve into a clean saucepan. Add the gorgonzola and whisk over low heat until combined. Season with a squeeze of lemon juice, and salt and pepper to taste.

Separate the silverbeet leaves from the stalks. Slice the stalks finely on an angle, so they are 4–5 cm long. Finely chop the leaves. Heat the oil in a large deep frying pan over high heat and sauté the stalks until just tender. Reduce the heat to medium. Add the gorgonzola cream and leaves. Cook until heated through and the leaves are tender.

Cook the gnocchi in the pot of boiling water in batches for 2–3 minutes, or just until they float to the top. Lift out with a slotted spoon and add to the gorgonzola mixture.

Check seasoning and consistency of sauce (thin with a little cream if too thick). Divide between serving plates or bowls and serve immediately.

CHEF'S NOTE

If you don't like silverbeet, then you can always mix it up and use spinach, beet leaves, or the ol' favourite, rocket. Finishing the gnocchi with some chopped herbs like fresh basil, oregano, or marjoram is pretty tasty too. Rainbow chard is simply silverbeet with stalks of different bright colours.

TO DRINK

Gewurztraminer is a sweet-flavoured dry wine often used to pair with the savouriness given by the gorgonzola here and the light bitterness of the silverbeet. Its delicate sourness will reset your palate for a delicious mouthful. Gewurztraminer is originally from northern Italy but great examples can be found in South Australia, providing the ripe texture you are looking for locally.

MARKET TIP

Using the correct potato is integral to obtaining a great result for gnocchi. If you can't find sebago, then you can always use king edward. Old 'floury' potatoes are best. Choose potatoes of a similar size so they take the same time to cook.

Braised Lentils, Confit Duck Leg, Pomegranate

Umami . Salty . Temperature

AUTUMN

STARTER

SERVES 6

seeds from 1 pomegranate
herbs to garnish, such as
   chervil, parsley and chives

CONFIT DUCK
6 duck legs
100 g sea salt
50 g sugar
few sprigs of thyme
2 bay leaves
10 black peppercorns
500 g duck fat, to cover

BRAISED LENTILS
500 g Australian green lentils
   or Puy lentils
1 bay leaf
1 sprig thyme
2 garlic cloves
1 celery stick, diced
½ carrot, diced
1 golden shallot, diced
50 g butter
25 ml olive oil
½ bunch parsley, leaves
   picked and chopped
sea salt

Puy lentils, the classic French variety, remind me of the colours and flavours of autumn more than anything else. Match them with slow-cooked duck legs and you have yourself a heart-warming meal that is a great one-pot wonder, perfect for sharing on cool autumnal days.

To make the confit duck, place the duck legs in a shallow glass or ceramic dish and cover with the combined salt, sugar, herbs and peppercorns. Place in the fridge to cure overnight.

Preheat the oven to 80°C. Rinse the legs and pat dry. Place in a roasting pan and cover with duck fat. Place in the oven to cook for 6–8 hours, until the meat is just falling off the bone.

Leave to cool in the fat, then remove the duck legs.

For the braised lentils, place the lentils in a sieve or colander and rinse under cold running water. Place in a large saucepan and add the herbs, garlic and vegetables. Cover with water and simmer over low heat for 20–30 minutes until soft and tender but not mushy. Remove from the heat and let cool in the liquid.

To serve, cook the duck legs in a frying pan over medium heat until the skin is lovely and crispy. Reheat the lentils in a saucepan. Add the butter, olive oil and parsley, and season with salt.

Place the lentils in a serving dish and arrange the crispy confit duck legs on top. Garnish with pomegranate seeds and herbs.

CHEF'S NOTE

If confit isn't your thing, or you don't have an excess of duck fat at home like we do at the restaurants, then slow braising the duck is a good option too. Another alternative is to buy good-quality confit duck legs already cooked and preserved. I have a favourite little French deli at the Queen Victoria Market that always looks after me with this kind of thing – normally the best come from France, in this case!

TO DRINK

A classic match with confit duck, a traditional dish from the south-west of France, would be a wine from the same region: madiran. This wine is mainly composed of tannat, producing deep and concentrated wines that match the generosity of the dish – the tannin will give energy to the pairing. I prefer it with a bit of age if possible.

MARKET TIP

Lentils are pretty much divided into two main categories, red and green, and it's important that you use the correct type for their intended use. Green lentils, also known as Puy lentils, and some Australian varietals work best for this dish. Red and yellow are better for dahl and soups and even as a dip or purée.

Suckling Pig Cooked on the Rotisserie

SERVES 20+

1 × 8 kg suckling pig
olive oil
sea salt
long rosemary sprigs
3 bunches baby carrots,
    trimmed and peeled
5 fennel bulbs, cut into wedges
40 baby kipfler
    potatoes, scrubbed
8 granny smith apples,
    quartered and cored
splash of cider vinegar
300 ml extra virgin olive oil
100 ml balsamic vinegar
1 clove garlic, cracked
4 heads radicchio
½ bunch flat-leaf parsley,
    leaves picked

BARBECUE SAUCE

3 teaspoons grapeseed oil
3 cloves garlic, chopped
1 golden shallot, finely sliced
¼ teaspoon ground ginger
¼ teaspoon allspice powder
¼ teaspoon mustard powder
¼ teaspoon cayenne pepper
¼ teaspoon smoked paprika
250 ml tomato passata
100 ml cider vinegar
120 g demerara sugar
1 tablespoon
    Worcestershire sauce
1 tablespoon golden syrup
½ teaspoon sea salt
¼ teaspoon freshly ground
    black pepper

I love suckling pig, particularly on the rotisserie – it's a way of cooking that is even and really gives a succulent finish to what you are cooking.

At least 2 hours before cooking (or the day before if possible), dry the pig skin with paper towel. Just before cooking, rub the pig with olive oil and a generous sprinkle of the salt. If you want to add aromatics to the salt such as mace, sage, peppercorns, fennel seeds then do so; they will certainly help impart flavour to the meat.

Prepare the fire for the rotisserie, making sure the coals are white and glowing before you start cooking.

Place the pig on the rod for the rotisserie and fasten securely.

Cook gently for 1 hour. Tie the rosemary sprigs to make a small brush. Dip in olive oil and brush the meat every 20 minutes as it cooks. Lower the rotisserie slightly and cook for a further 3 hours or until crispy, golden and delicious, continuing to brush the skin with oil as before.

To make the barbecue sauce, heat the oil in a small saucepan over low heat. Cook the garlic and shallot until tender but not coloured. Add the spices and toast gently for a minute, then add the rest of the ingredients and simmer for 20 minutes. Cool slightly then transfer to a blender and blitz until smooth. Pass through a fine sieve, check seasoning and chill until needed.

When you are about half an hour off serving, place the carrots, fennel wedges, potatoes and apple in a large roasting pan and drizzle with olive oil. Toss to coat, season with salt then spread out evenly. Roast on the base of the rotisserie underneath the pig for 25 minutes, until golden and tender. When nearly cooked add a splash of cider vinegar and a splash more olive oil.

Mix the 300 ml extra virgin olive oil, balsamic vinegar and garlic clove in a large bowl. Roll the radicchio through it. Place a grillplate over the coals. Place the radicchio on the grillplate and cook until the leaves start to char. Peel the leaves off as they cook, exposing the leaves underneath. Keep repeating so you have delicious charred leaves. Mix the charred leaves with the roasted vegetables and parsley leaves, and dress lightly with the remaining vinaigrette.

Break the suckling pig down before serving with the vegetables and barbecue sauce.

CHEF'S NOTE

This is a special occasion dish, that's for sure! It takes time and care to ensure best results. If you don't have a fire pit, rotisserie or a massive barbecue for the suckling pig, then slow-roasted pork shoulder is also a winner, especially with the barbecue sauce!

TO DRINK

A subtle pinot noir from Victoria is the regional pick here. I would choose a pinot from a higher altitude vineyard with freshness and vibrant fruits. The Yarra Valley or Macedon Ranges are good choices for their light texture but firm tannins that will balance the fondant flesh of the pig. A bit of age here can give an extra earthy flavour, adding another dimension to the match.

MARKET TIP

Suckling pigs can be a bit hard to source sometimes, so make sure that you have a good chat to your butcher and preorder it within plenty of time. My favourite supplier is Western Plains Pork, a family-run, free-range pork farm about 150 km west of Melbourne in Mount Mercer. The best size is somewhere within the 8–10 kg range.

Grass-fed T-Bone, Creamed Kale, Black Garlic

SERVES 2–3

1 × 1.2 kg grass-fed
   T-bone steak
2 bunches kale,
   stalks removed
350 ml double cream
2 sprigs thyme
¼ cup olive oil
sea salt
freshly ground black pepper
6 golden shallots, finely sliced
2 bulbs black garlic, crushed
   to a paste
½ lemon (optional)

Grass-fed, grain-fed or wagyu? That's the most common question I'm asked when discussing meat. I always have been, and always will be, a grass-fed man: I love the flavour and the texture. Grain-fed is normally a more consistent product, especially during the winter months, and great wagyu is hard to beat, so it's really all about budget and personal preference.

Remove the steak from the fridge about 20 minutes before cooking. Bring a large saucepan of salted water to the boil. Preheat a barbecue grillplate on high.

Prepare a large bowl of iced water. Blanch the kale in the boiling water for about 1½ minutes, until tender. Drain well and plunge into the ice water to stop it cooking. Drain again, squeeze out the excess water and roughly chop.

Put the cream and thyme into a small saucepan over medium heat. Simmer until reduced by two-thirds. Take off the heat and set aside.

Rub the steak with a little of the olive oil and season well with salt and pepper. Cook on the barbecue for 4–5 minutes each side. Keep in mind that the fillet part of the steak will cook more quickly, so to keep it moist position the steak with the striploin over the hotter part of the barbecue. (Alternatively, cook the steak in a frying pan over high heat for 4–5 minutes each side.) Cover the steak loosely with foil and set aside in a warm place to rest for 10 minutes.

While the meat is resting, heat the remaining oil in a heavy-based frying pan over medium heat. Add the shallot and cook, without colouring, until tender. Add the garlic paste to the pan and stir to dissolve. Add the chopped kale and season well. When it is hot add the reduced cream and toss to coat well. Season with a squeeze of lemon juice if you think it is needed.

Slice the meat off the bone and serve with the creamed kale, drizzled with any extra reduced cream from the pan.

CHEF'S NOTE

When buying T-bone steaks always look for ones with tenderloins the same thickness as the striploin. If the steaks are cut from yearling beef, which are relatively small cattle, the short loins are small, resulting in a consistent thickness to both parts of the steak. Grass-fed beef has a wonderful flavour and texture. It may not achieve the high marbling of grain-fed beef but the fat it has is truly delicious.

TO DRINK

A cabernet sauvignon with its typical pepperiness and Indian ink flavours will balance out the generosity of this dish and intensity of the flavours. It calls for a deep wine with enough length to accompany the sweet intense black garlic. Great examples are found in the Margaret River in Western Australia or for a richer style look to the Napa Valley, California.

MARKET TIP

If you can find it, it's always better to purchase dry-aged steak. Even a week makes a huge difference – it firms up the meat, intensifies the flavour and really elevates your meat to the next level. This recipe uses one large steak cut to serve 2–3.

SERVES 4

250 g blanched almonds
sea salt
freshly ground black pepper
4 × 400 g rock flathead,
    scaled, cleaned,
    heads removed
50 ml vegetable oil
200 g butter
250 g seedless white grapes,
    cut in half lengthways
50 ml sherry vinegar
finely grated zest and juice
    of 1 lemon
2 tablespoons chopped
    flat-leaf parsley

Growing up I spent many weekends down the Mornington Peninsula, and fished the bay pretty regularly. Our most common catch was flathead. I don't think I really appreciated the delicate, sweet flesh at the time, but I sure do now!

Preheat the oven to 180°C. Spread the almonds on a baking tray and bake for 4–6 minutes, until golden. Transfer to a plate to cool.

Season the fish with salt and pepper. Heat the vegetable oil in 2 large frying pans over medium heat. Add the fish and cook gently for 8–10 minutes, turning every 2–3 minutes, until just cooked.

Remove the fish from the pan and place on a warm tray, loosely covered with foil, in a warm place to rest while you make the sauce.

Melt the butter in a frying pan and just when it starts foaming add the almonds. When the butter starts to brown, add the grapes, sherry vinegar, lemon zest and juice, and parsley. Place the fish on a serving platter and cover with the sauce.

CHEF'S NOTE

Fish is always best roasted on the bone: it stays juicier and keeps a better shape. Don't be worried about roasting whole, or partially attached to the bone; it just means you need to be careful when eating so you don't swallow any little pin bones.

TO DRINK

A good-quality pinot blanc here with discreet and subtle notes to support the dish and respect the delicate balance. An Alsacian-style pinot blanc will show enough texture to underline the flesh of the fish and bring enough acidity to match the grapes. The subtle aromas will let the delicate almonds shine in this dish.

MARKET TIP

These days grapes are readily available in the supermarket most of the year, but they are best when just ripe and ready for the plucking around the 'vintage' point. That's when winemakers are processing their grapes, or the next 'vintage' of wine, just when I like to cook with them – sweet and juicy!

Braised Rabbit, Apricots, Witlof

SERVES 4–6

2 large farmed rabbits, jointed
sea salt
freshly ground black pepper
plain flour, for dusting
1 tablespoon vegetable oil
5 cloves garlic, finely sliced
100 g smoked pancetta, diced
2 carrots, diced
2 celery sticks, diced
2 brown onions, diced
300 ml dry white wine
500 ml chicken stock
2 sprigs thyme
1 sprig tarragon
1 bay leaf
150 g dried apricots
50 ml olive oil
3 heads witlof,
    halved lengthways
knob of butter
1 tablespoon
    wholegrain mustard
1 sprig tarragon, extra,
    leaves picked
½ lemon (optional)

'Underground chicken', that's what my grandmother used to call rabbit. It's quite a versatile protein that is great braised, roasted or made into rillettes. Here, the apricots add a sweetness and the witlof (also known as Belgian endive) brings some bitterness, a perfect balance! Some couscous would work well as a side with this dish, or a classic *pommes boulangères* rich with onions and thyme (page 173).

Preheat the oven to 150°C. Season the rabbit pieces and dust with flour, shaking off the excess.

Heat the vegetable oil in a large heavy-based ovenproof pot over medium–high heat. Cook the rabbit pieces, turning occasionally, until golden all over. Set aside.

Reduce the heat to low and gently fry the garlic until soft. Add the pancetta and cook until lightly browned. Add the vegetables and a good pinch of salt and cook, stirring occasionally, until soft but not coloured.

Pour over the white wine and increase the heat to medium. Cook until reduced by two-thirds. Add the stock and the herbs and bring to a simmer. Add the apricots and rabbit to the pan, cover with a lid and bake in the oven for about 1½ hours, until the meat is tender. Remove from the oven and rest the meat in the pan for 10 minutes.

Heat the olive oil in a frying pan over medium heat. Add the witlof to the pan cut-side down and cook until caramelised. Turn and caramelise the other side.

Strain off the excess oil from the pan. Add a ladleful of the cooking liquid from the rabbit and the butter. Cook, turning the witlof occasionally, for 6–8 minutes to glaze so it becomes shiny and rich.

Remove the rabbit from the pot. Remove the loins and saddle meat from the bone. Bring the liquid in the pot to a simmer over medium-low heat. Stir in the mustard and extra tarragon leaves, and check the seasoning. Add a squeeze of lemon juice if needed.

Place the rabbit on a serving plate and, with a spoon, use the liquid to glaze it. Serve with the glazed witlof alongside.

CHEF'S NOTE

Usually as chefs we like to use fresh ingredients, but the dried apricots really make a difference to this dish: they soak up all the juices and hold their shape better than fresh ones would.

TO DRINK

You'll want a textural white here with lots of character. My choice is a wine based on the grenache blanc grape variety – some of the best examples are from Chateauneuf du Pape, in the Rhône Valley. More popular in the red version, a white Chateauneuf will suggest spice and nutty flavour to pair with the generosity of this dish.

MARKET TIP

Farmed rabbit is pretty consistent these days that's for sure, but if you like your meat to be a little bit 'gamier', then ask your butcher if they have any wild ones – you'll be surprised by the difference in flavour and texture.

King Salmon, Jerusalem Artichoke, Verjus

Umami . Bitter . Texture

SERVES 4

1 kg Jerusalem
    artichokes, washed
sprig of thyme
5 cloves garlic, peeled
    and halved
1 bay leaf
sea salt
100 ml olive oil
4 × 150 king salmon portions,
    scaled and pin boned
freshly ground black pepper
100 g butter

VERJUS BEURRE BLANC
1 golden shallot, finely sliced
1 clove garlic, crushed
6 black peppercorns
1 star anise
1 bay leaf
250 ml verjus
125 ml white wine
120 g cold unsalted butter, diced
1 tablespoon lemon juice
sea salt
100 g seedless white grapes
1 tablespoon chopped tarragon

There is a world of difference between farmed Atlantic salmon and king salmon. The king salmon has a wonderful full colour and amazingly high fat content, which makes for fantastic eating both texturally and flavour-wise. Most we have access to originates in the Marlborough region of New Zealand.

Preheat the oven to 175°C. Drop the Jerusalem artichokes into a large pan of boiling salted water and cook for 5 minutes. Drain. Lay a large sheet of foil on a baking tray. Place the artichokes on the foil and add the thyme, garlic and bay leaf. Season with salt and seal tightly so no steam can escape. Reduce oven heat to 160°C and bake for about 45 minutes, or until tender.

To make the verjus beurre blanc, combine the shallot, garlic, peppercorns, star anise and bay leaf in a small saucepan. Add the verjus and wine and bring to a simmer over medium heat. Cook until reduced to about 2 tablespoons. Reduce the heat to low and add the butter a few pieces at a time, whisking constantly. Make sure the butter has completely combined and the mixture is smooth before adding more butter. Add the lemon juice and season to taste. Strain into a bowl and keep warm.

To cook the fish, heat half the olive oil in a large ovenproof frying pan over medium–high heat. Season the fish portions with salt and pepper. Place the fish in the pan skin-side down, and reduce heat to medium. Cook for 3–4 minutes, until the skin has caramelised and starts to crisp up. Transfer the pan to the oven and cook for another 3–4 minutes, until the flesh is cooked through. The fish is not turned during cooking, ensuring crisp skin and moist flesh. Remove from the oven and place back on the stove over medium heat. Add 50 g of the butter and baste the fish as the butter foams. Add a good squeeze of lemon juice and remove from the pan.

Meanwhile, heat the remaining oil and butter in a large frying pan and add the artichokes. Cook, tossing to coat, until golden and crispy.

Warm the beurre blanc again, add the grapes and tarragon and serve.

CHEF'S NOTE

I always like to cook fatty, oily fish like salmon 'under' – that is, a little bit on the rare side. Salmon is perfect for this and is best eaten rare–medium rare. It doesn't dry out and is really at its peak.

TO DRINK

This is a dish with big flavours, giving the opportunity to offer a red wine as a companion. The generosity of the salmon paired with the earthiness of the Jerusalem artichoke call for the flavours of a glass of poulsard from the Jura region, offering little red berries and earthy notes.

MARKET TIP

It's a bit painful, but spend the time when choosing Jerusalem artichokes to ensure you 'grade' them for size – if they are a nice consistent size, then they cook more evenly.

SERVES 6

grapeseed oil, to deep-fry,
  plus extra
1 bunch kale
sea salt, to season
1 × 200 g piece pancetta
2 red onions, finely diced
1 green apple, peeled,
  finely diced
3 cloves garlic, thinly sliced
200 g kalettes, halved
  lengthways, stems trimmed
½ bunch flat-leaf parsley,
  leaves chopped
1 tablespoon chopped
  thyme leaves
freshly ground black pepper
¼ cup apple cider vinegar
1 × 200 g piece manchego

Kalettes, or kale sprouts: a cross between kale and brussels sprouts, they were developed in the mid '90s in England and only recently brought to market in Australia. Kalettes were cross-bred using techniques that are old enough to be called 'traditional'. So, when you see kalettes or grapefruit or broccolini (yes, broccolini) and other new fruit and vegetables on your grocer's shelf, do a little research. Take a risk. The truth is, they're just really tasty.

Pour 250 ml grapeseed oil into a large pot and heat to 180°C. Meanwhile, tear the kale leaves from the stems and break into large pieces. Wash and dry thoroughly.

Working in 4 batches, quickly drop the kale into the oil and immediately cover the pot with a lid. You must put the lid on in almost the same motion as you drop in the leaves to prevent the oil from spitting up and potentially causing a burn. Once the popping noise stops, scoop out the kale chips onto a baking tray lined with paper towel. Season with salt. Once cool, store in an airtight container for up to 2 days.

Preheat the oven to 180°C. Cut the pancetta into 1.5 cm cubes (these are called lardons). Heat a frying pan over medium heat and pour enough grapeseed oil into the pan so it is 3 mm deep. Add the lardons to the pan and increase the heat to high. Cook for a few minutes, tossing often so they brown evenly on all sides. Transfer to a bowl lined with paper towel to drain.

Drain most of the oil from the pan into a small bowl and set aside. Reduce heat to low. Add the onion to the pan and season with a small amount of salt. Cook the onion gently until it becomes translucent and releases liquid, then add the apple and garlic. Cook gently until the apple is soft and the garlic is translucent.

Meanwhile, preheat a large ovenproof frying pan over high heat with the reserved oil. Once the pan is nearly smoking, add the kalettes to the pan, cut-side down. Cook until evenly browned, then flip the kalettes and transfer the pan to the oven. Cook for 4–5 minutes, until al dente.

Tip the kalettes into a large mixing bowl. Add the onion and apple mixture, the lardons, parsley and thyme. Season with salt and pepper and drizzle with the apple cider vinegar. Place the mixture into a serving bowl and garnish with the kale chips. Using a vegetable peeler, shave large strips of manchego over the top to garnish.

CHEF'S NOTE

It is easy to be put off by the state of modern agriculture these days. Between GMOs, pesticides and aggressive corporate expansion, it's hard to know what is safe, wholesome or even politically correct to serve and eat. But things like kalettes are one of the definite upsides of agriculture today.

MARKET TIP

I like to use a smoked pancetta, but if you don't have any, then a really good streaky bacon is a good substitute. Manchego is a Spanish cheese available from most good delis.

Coal-roasted Cabbage, Buttermilk, Sumac

SERVES 8

2 small red cabbages
olive oil
sea salt
nasturtium leaves and flowers,
   to garnish

SUMAC OIL
2 tablespoons ground sumac
120 ml grapeseed oil

BUTTERMILK DRESSING
½ teaspoon star anise
1 teaspoon coriander seeds
1 teaspoon smoked paprika
pinch of chilli powder
300 ml buttermilk
3 teaspoons lime juice
finely grated zest of 2 limes
½ teaspoon of salt

This is a very simple dish – the most important ingredient is heat. And for building a very hot fire, the very best charcoal is Japanese binchotan charcoal. It requires patience. You must start your fire far in advance; it will take a very long time (and potentially a lot of kindling) to get started. As it heats up, it will begin to splinter and make loud cracking noises as the wood tempers. It may even suddenly burst from the heat all of a sudden with a loud noise that sounds simultaneously like a small explosion and like a piece of glass clinking another – it is startling but safe. But once it gets hot, this is the hottest charcoal I know of and it burns the longest. You can find it at your local Japanese importer.

To make the sumac oil, combine the sumac and grapeseed oil in a blender and blend on high for 1–2 minutes. The oil will look grainy and slightly purple in color. Pour into a jar, cover, and refrigerate overnight for the flavours to infuse.

For the buttermilk dressing, place the star anise and coriander seeds in a frying pan over medium heat. Cook for a few minutes, until quite aromatic and brown. Transfer to a plate to cool, then place in a spice grinder and blitz into a fine powder. Pass the powder through a sieve in order to remove any large woody pieces. Combine with the other ingredients, stirring until smooth. Cover and refrigerate until needed (it will keep for up to 2 days).

Remove and discard the outer leaves of the cabbages, down to the bright red, youthful leaves, and cut the cabbages into quarters. Trim away the cores, drizzle with olive oil and season generously with salt.

Build a medium-sized fire in a barbecue pit or a woodfired oven. Wrap each quarter of cabbage in foil. Wait for the fire to die down to embers and bury the cabbage among the coals. Let them roast for 10–15 minutes. The cabbage will begin to wilt and take on a strong smoky flavour. Alternatively, char the cabbage on a hot grillplate, then wrap in foil and cook in a 200°C oven for 15 minutes.

Remove the parcels from the heat and unwrap. Transfer the cabbage to a serving platter and spoon over the buttermilk dressing and sumac oil. Garnish with nasturtium leaves and petals.

CHEF'S NOTE

Nothing beats the flavour of wood or charcoal, and where possible try to use it for the cabbage – if cooking with binchotan isn't possible, you'll need a barbecue you can build a fire with deep coals in – not a regular gas barbecue. Having said that, if you don't have a fire pit or charcoal, you still get pretty good results by wrapping this cabbage in tin foil and baking it in a hot oven . . . it's not the same, but still not bad!

MARKET TIP

I like to use red cabbages for this as they have a 'meatier' flavour than other varieties. But it's nice to mix things up sometimes too, so why not try savoy cabbage or even wombok?

Roast Cauliflower, Chickpeas, Tahini

SERVES 8

2 medium cauliflowers
olive oil, to drizzle
sea salt
250 g raisins
250 g pecans, toasted
    and chopped
10 g ras el hanout
½ bunch mint, leaves chopped
½ bunch flat-leaf parsley,
    leaves chopped
extra mint and parsley,
    to garnish

TAHINI DRESSING
130 g tahini
250 g plain yoghurt
100 ml olive oil
30 ml lemon juice
15 g ground cumin
sea salt, to season

FRIED CHICKPEAS
grapeseed oil, to deep-fry
1 × 400 g can chickpeas,
    rinsed and drained
sea salt

Everyone seems to be eating more veggies these days, and when you can have things like whole roasted cauliflower that's 'meaty' in its own right, why wouldn't you? The raisins add a touch of sweetness, ras el hanout some aromatic spice, the pecans cover the 'nuttiness', and a sharp dressing from the tahini and yoghurt complete the quadrella.

To make the tahini dressing, combine the tahini, yoghurt, olive oil, lemon juice and cumin in a mixing bowl and season with salt. Cover and refrigerate until needed (it will keep for up to 1 week).

For the fried chickpeas, pour enough grapeseed oil into a medium saucepan so it is just under half full. Heat over medium heat to 150°C. Pat the drained chickpeas dry with paper towels. Place half the chickpeas in the oil and cook for a few minutes, until golden brown. Using a small metal sieve, remove the chickpeas from the oil and transfer to a baking tray lined with paper towel. Season with salt and repeat with the remaining chickpeas. This should be done on the day you serve the salad, as the chickpeas lose their crunch quickly.

Preheat the oven to 230°C. Trim and discard the leaves from the cauliflowers and wash thoroughly. Dry the cauliflowers with paper towel, then coat with olive oil and season with salt. Place the cauliflowers on a wire rack in a large roasting pan. Roast until the outside is a deep brown. It shouldn't take long – begin checking after 15 minutes.

Set the cauliflowers aside to cool. Cut each cauliflower in half and remove the core. Using your hands, break into large florets.

Place the cauliflower into a large mixing bowl. Add the raisins, pecans, ras el hanout, mint, parsley and two-thirds of the fried chickpeas. Dress with a very liberal amount of the tahini dressing (it should look creamy) and season with salt.

Transfer the mixture to a serving bowl and garnish with mint, parsley and remaining fried chickpeas.

CHEF'S NOTE
Roasting cauliflower whole is a slightly different method, but is pretty easy and provides excellent results. The cauliflower keeps its shape and caramelises evenly.

MARKET TIP
While it's pretty much a warm salad, this recipe would also make a wonderful hot side dish – even a gratin that is served alongside roast pork or whole fish.

Curried Pumpkin Mash,
Herb Salad

Texture . Bitter . Sour . Spicy

SERVES 8

250 g butter
2 medium butternut pumpkins
sea salt
2 tablespoons curry powder
¼ cup pumpkin seeds
　(pepitas), toasted
½ cup flat-leaf parsley leaves
½ cup celery leaves
½ cup carrot tops (optional)
½ witlof, leaves separated

PUMPKIN DRESSING
100 ml pumpkin seed oil
50 ml olive oil
50 ml champagne vinegar
1 clove garlic, finely chopped
1 golden shallot,
　finely chopped

As chefs we always look for a bit of texture in a dish – some crunch certainly does make the eating experience a whole lot better. The salad we serve with this pumpkin mash does just that: it lightens up the dish, adds some texture and the acid helps cut through the richness of the buttery mash.

To make the pumpkin dressing, combine the pumpkin seed oil, olive oil and champagne vinegar in a small bowl. Add the garlic and shallot and whisk to combine. Cover and refrigerate until needed (it will keep for up to 2 days).

Place the butter in a saucepan over medium heat. Cook the butter until brown (145°C is the perfect temperature for brown butter). Pass it through a fine sieve into a mixing bowl. Reserve.

Meanwhile, remove the top and bottom from each pumpkin, and cut off the skin. Cut the flesh into small cubes and discard the seeds and membrane. Place in a large steamer basket over a pan of boiling water (or cook in batches if your steamer is small). Cook for 10 minutes or until tender but not mushy – be careful to leave some texture or it will turn to a purée before your very eyes.

Transfer the pumpkin to a large bowl. Add the curry powder and 150 ml of the brown butter. Season with salt, and use a potato masher to mash until smooth. The result should be a rich, buttery mash. Feel free to add all the brown butter if that is to your taste!

In another small mixing bowl combine the pumpkin seeds, parsley, celery, carrot tops and witlof. Dress the salad with pumpkin dressing to taste. Serve alongside the mash, or divide the mash onto plates and top with a small heap of salad to cut through the richness.

CHEF'S NOTE

Add as much or as little butter as you like, depending on your diet and tastebuds. I always like plenty, but with a pumpkin mash, unlike a potato mash, you can get away with making it a bit 'healthier' if you desire!

MARKET TIP

Like potatoes, different pumpkins have different uses and strengths. Butternut is a great all-rounder, Queensland blue is brilliant for baking, Kent or jap pumpkin is fantastic for soups, while jarrahdale, one of the most common, is perfect for steaming or boiling.

Soft Polenta, Mushrooms, Soft Egg

SERVES 6

MUSHROOM STOCK
grapeseed oil
500 g button mushrooms,
    cleaned, and halved if large
2 litres chicken
250 ml apple juice
50 ml brandy
5 sprigs thyme
5 black peppercorns

SOFT EGGS
6 eggs
100 ml white vinegar
salt

POLENTA
170 g fine yellow polenta
1 bunch flat-leaf parsley,
    leaves chopped
125 g mascarpone
40 g parmesan, finely grated,
    plus extra to serve
½ lemon
sea salt
freshly ground black pepper

MUSHROOMS
700 g enoki mushrooms,
    cleaned
grapeseed oil
100 g butter, softened
10 cloves garlic
½ bunch thyme

Soft, creamy, polenta is a delicious savoury kind of porridge that I'd happily eat every day for breakfast in mushroom season! The soft egg adds a wonderful luxuriousness to this dish, and the earthiness and umami of the mushrooms makes it to die for.

To make the mushroom stock, preheat a stockpot over high heat. Add a thin film of grapeseed oil to the bottom of the pot, about 2 mm deep. Add just enough of the mushrooms to mostly cover the bottom of the pan. Don't try to cook all of the mushrooms at once or they won't colour.

Sauté for 3–4 minutes or until golden. Remove from the pot and repeat with the remaining mushrooms in batches. Return all the mushrooms to the pot. Add the chicken stock, apple juice, brandy, thyme and peppercorns. Bring to a simmer over medium heat. Cook uncovered until the stock has reduced by half. Strain and cool. This stock will keep in the fridge for 3–4 days, and it freezes very well.

To cook the eggs, combine the vinegar with 1.5 litres water in a large saucepan. Add a good pinch of salt and bring to the boil. Crack the eggs into separate small ramekins. Using a wooden spoon, stir the water to create a whirlpool. Working one at a time, carefully slide an egg into the pot, ensuring it is rotating around the pan, which gives a great shape. Cook for 2 minutes, remove with a slotted spoon and place in iced water to stop the cooking. When cold, remove from the water. Repeat with remaining eggs and set aside until required.

For the polenta, bring 750 ml of the mushroom stock to a simmer in a medium saucepan over medium heat, and stream in the polenta, whisking as you go. Reduce the heat to low and continue to cook, stirring, for 15 minutes. Stir in the parsley, mascarpone and parmesan. Season the polenta with a squeeze of lemon juice, salt and pepper.

For the mushrooms, trim the bottoms from the enoki but keep them attached at the stem end, and slice into 1 cm thick enoki mushroom 'bundles'. Preheat a large frying pan over high heat. Add enough grapeseed oil to coat the bottom of the pan and heat so it is almost smoking. Working in batches, carefully place the enoki in and do not move them until they are nicely brown.

Flip the mushrooms quickly, add a heaped tablespoon of butter, 1 clove garlic and 2 sprigs thyme to the pan. Coat the mushrooms in this butter, season with salt and pepper, then drain on a paper towel. Repeat, adding more butter, garlic and thyme with each batch.

To serve, reheat all the eggs in a pot of simmering water for 1–2 minutes. If the polenta has thickened and needs loosening up, simply stir in a little hot mushroom stock. Spoon onto serving plates and top with the mushrooms and eggs. Garnish with a little extra grated parmesan.

CHEF'S NOTE

This is a perfect side dish for those nights in autumn when it starts to get cooler, but make the portion a little bigger and it's a perfect entrée or meal in itself. To clean the pine mushrooms, simply use a dry paper towel (or a clean soft sponge) to wipe away any dirt. Use a pair of tweezers to remove any dirt or pine needles found in the gills.

MARKET TIP

Try and utilise the short season of wild mushrooms we have in Australia to enjoy the beautiful pine mushrooms, slippery jacks, grey ghosts and the rare morel. If not around, the cultivated mushroom options are extensive these days too.

Poached Quince Clafoutis, Honey Ice-cream, Honeycomb

AUTUMN

DESSERT

SERVES 4–6

POACHED QUINCE
2 large quinces
650 g caster sugar
2 star anise
1 cinnamon stick
8 cloves
10 black peppercorns
1 vanilla bean, split,
    seeds scraped
juice and peel (in wide strips)
    of 1 lemon

HONEY ICE-CREAM
600 ml milk
400 ml cream
160 g honey
200 g egg yolks (about 10)
190 g caster sugar

CLAFOUTIS
soft butter, to grease
1½ tablespoons plain flour
40 g ground almonds
85 g caster sugar
2 eggs
4 egg yolks
220 g mascarpone
chopped walnuts, to serve
honeycomb, to serve

I remember when I was an apprentice and I cooked my first quince. Actually, we pinched them from a tree in a vacant block not far from the restaurant, and I had no idea what they were or how to cook them! Boy, was I in for a treat. A clafoutis is really a French pudding, a batter-like mix that makes a perfect hot dessert.

To poach the quinces, peel and quarter each quince and remove the cores. Wrap the peel and cores in muslin and tie into a bundle. Combine the sugar, spices, lemon juice and peel in a large saucepan. Add the quince quarters and the muslin bundle, and pour in 1.2 litres water. Cover and bring to the boil, then reduce the heat to very low and simmer for 3½–4 hours, until the quince pieces are soft and sticky. Turn the heat off and allow the quince to cool in the syrup. Use a slotted spoon to lift the quince quarters from the syrup. Slice the quince lengthways and fan out.

To make the honey ice-cream, combine the milk, cream and honey in a medium saucepan and bring to a low simmer over medium heat. Meanwhile, whisk the egg yolks and sugar in an electric mixer until pale and thick. Add one-third of the milk mixture to the yolk mixture and whisk to combine. Pour back into the pan with the remaining milk mixture. Stir over low heat until thickened (until a thermometer reaches 83°C). Pass the mixture through a fine sieve into a bowl. Stand the bowl in a larger bowl of ice and stir to release the heat. Once cooled, churn in an ice-cream machine. Transfer to an airtight container and freeze.

For the clafoutis, whisk the flour, ground almonds, sugar, eggs, yolks and mascarpone until smooth. Set aside at room temperature to rest for 1 hour.

Preheat the oven to 230°C. Grease a 20 cm × 20 cm × 5 cm pan lightly with butter (I've used an ovenproof frying pan here but a ceramic baking dish is fine). Pour the batter into the prepared dish and place the quince slices on top. Bake for 10–12 minutes, until golden, slightly risen and bouncy to touch. Stand for 1–2 minutes before serving.

To serve, sprinkle the hot clafoutis with chopped walnuts and chunks of honeycomb. Place a generous scoop of honey ice-cream on top of each serving.

CHEF'S NOTE

A clafoutis is classically made with cherries, but if you don't have any (or any quinces) then you can always use apricots, plums, or last season's preserved berries. You could replace the honey ice-cream with a good-quality purchased vanilla ice-cream, if you prefer.

TO DRINK

Another of the most popular grape varieties for the production of sweet wine is chenin blanc. Produced all around the world from America to South Africa, probably the best examples are bottled in the Loire Valley, France.

MARKET TIP

Choose firm, fragrant quinces. Admittedly they are a little tedious to prepare, but the end result of these slow-cooked ruby-red diamonds is a real treat. They are great with muesli for brekkie too, or even just with natural yoghurt.

Warm Chocolate and Chestnut Puddings

SERVES 6

soft butter, to grease
cocoa powder, to dust
125 g unsalted butter, chopped
125 g dark chocolate
   (70%), chopped
225 g chestnut purée
100 ml milk
2 eggs, separated
75 g caster sugar
icing sugar, to dust
double cream, to serve

Warm chocolate puddings . . . decadent, luxurious and a naughty treat! Such a crowd-pleasing favourite, these puddings are an all-time classic that you must add to your repertoire. The addition of chestnuts takes them to yet another level.

Preheat the oven to 170°C. Generously grease six 150 ml capacity dariole moulds with butter. Sprinkle a tablespoon of cocoa powder into a ramekin and roll around so the cocoa powder coats the inside evenly. Shake out the excess into the next ramekin. Alternatively, this can be made as a sharing dish in one large 1 litre capacity ceramic baking dish.

Combine the butter and chocolate in a heatproof bowl over a saucepan of simmering water (the base of the bowl should not touch the water). Melt over medium heat, then stir until smooth. Remove from the heat.

Combine the chestnut purée and milk in a saucepan and heat over low heat, whisking until smooth. Remove from the heat and set aside. In a separate bowl, use electric beaters to beat the egg yolks with the sugar until pale and fluffy. Stir the chocolate and butter mixture into the chestnut and milk mixture until evenly combined. Add all of this to the yolk mixture, and fold in to make a smooth batter.

Whisk the egg whites in a clean bowl until medium peaks form. Add to the chocolate mixture in 3 batches, folding gently to combine. Pour into the prepared ramekins and stand them on a baking tray. Bake for 12–15 minutes, until puffed and the tops have cracked. Remove from the oven and allow to cool for 2–3 minutes. If using a large baking dish, cook for 25–30 minutes.

Serve hot dusted with icing sugar, topped with a dollop of double cream.

CHEF'S NOTE

It's always important to try to buy the best chocolate you can afford. Also worth noting is that the higher the percentage of the cacao in the chocolate, the less sugar and more cacao solids. So semi sweet is 50–62%, bittersweet 63–72% and anything over 73% is extra bittersweet.

TO DRINK

Fortified red wine and port are a match made in heaven here as the chestnut component adds richness and texture, which are amazing. Choose a wine showing complexity and more integrated sweetness. Colheita Port from Portugal, Très Vieux Pineau des Charentes from France, Commandaria from Greece . . .

MARKET TIP

I like to use fresh, roasted chestnuts when in season – it's best to roast them over an open flame, carefully peel them then make a purée in a food processor or blender. If you don't have the time or the patience for this, a good quality canned chestnut purée is a solid substitute.

Stewed Apricots, Chamomile Rice Pudding

SERVES 8-10

STEWED APRICOTS
3 chamomile tea bags
250 ml white verjus
750 ml water
300 g dried apricots
4 star anise
1 vanilla bean, split,
    seeds scraped

CHAMOMILE RICE PUDDING
500 ml milk
1 vanilla bean, split,
    seeds scraped
500 ml water
¼ cup dried chamomile flowers
50 g butter, plus extra to serve
120 g arborio rice
80 g caster sugar
pinch of salt
120 ml cream

When I was a kid, I used to always sneak a can of creamed rice into the shopping trolley. I loved the stuff! My version of rice pudding is a little healthier (not much!) and more refined than that stuff, but just as delicious – maybe even more so.

For the stewed apricots, place the tea bags, verjus and water into a saucepan and bring to the boil. Turn off the heat and leave to steep for 10 minutes. Remove the tea bags and add the apricots, star anise and vanilla bean and seeds to the pan. Bring to the boil, then reduce the heat to low and simmer for 30–45 minutes, until the apricots are tender and the liquid has reduced and is syrupy. Set aside to cool.

To make the chamomile rice pudding, place the milk in a small saucepan with the vanilla bean and seeds and warm over low heat. Place the water in another small saucepan and add the chamomile flowers. Heat over low heat, and steep for at least 10 minutes. Strain the flowers through a fine sieve and return the chamomile water to a clean pan to keep warm.

Melt the butter in a wide saucepan over medium heat. Add the rice and stir to coat in the butter. Cook for just a minute until the rice starts to turn toasty and nutty. Use a ladle to add the chamomile water little by little to the rice, stirring constantly and adding more liquid only when it has been absorbed, just as you would when making risotto. Once you have used all the water, switch to the vanilla milk, adding gradually and stirring.

Once the pudding has reached a thick, porridge-like texture (this will take 25–30 minutes), add the sugar and a pinch of salt. Stir to dissolve. Take the pan off the heat and stir in the cream.

To serve, ladle the warm rice pudding into serving bowls, add a small knob of butter and top with stewed apricots. Drizzle generously with the syrup.

CHEF'S NOTE
I have slow-cooked and stewed the apricots in this recipe, but if you have some dry ones around, 'poaching' or just pouring the hot syrup onto them so they swell up is a great way to use any dried fruit that's kicking about. You can add cardamom when stewing them for extra spice, too. The rice pudding is best served warm but is also delicious cold.

TO DRINK
A German riesling from the Mosel region with a spätlese style is perfect with apricots. These grapes are usually harvested just after the normal harvest so that the dry grape keeps a freshness and vibrancy, which will go along with delicate flavours such as the chamomile. The light spritz traditionally felt at the opening will balance the creaminess of the rice pudding.

MARKET TIP
Different rice has different uses. I find that good-quality arborio works best for the rice pudding, and make sure you don't undercook the rice as there is nothing worse than chalky, crunchy pudding!

Caramel Roasted Pears, Armagnac and Date Ice-Cream

SERVES 4-6

DATE PUREE
250 g medjool dates, pitted
350 ml water
100 g icing sugar
finely grated zest of ¼ orange
1 teaspoon bicarbonate of soda

ARMAGNAC AND DATE
ICE-CREAM
250 ml milk
250 ml thickened cream
1 vanilla bean, split,
    seeds scraped
8 egg yolks
130 g caster sugar
1½ tablespoons Armagnac

CARAMEL ROASTED PEARS
8 under-ripe bartlett
    or william pears
lemon juice
600 g caster sugar
150 ml water
¼ cup Armagnac
pinch of salt

Apples, pears, who cares? Anything in a caramel syrup splashed with Armagnac must be a winner – and this dish is no exception. Simple yet elegant, it's a classic flavour combo that hits the spot. You're welcome to add any warm spices to the caramel for the pears such as cinnamon, star anise, cloves or nutmeg – it's totally up to you.

To make the date purée, combine the dates, water, icing sugar, zest and bicarbonate of soda in a saucepan. Bring to the boil over medium heat and cook until the water has evaporated and the dates have broken down to a pulp. Cool slightly, then transfer to a food processor and process until smooth. Cover and set aside.

To make the ice-cream, place the milk, cream, vanilla bean and seeds in a saucepan and heat to 80°C (just below boiling point). Combine the egg yolks and sugar in a mixing bowl and whisk until pale and creamy. Pour the hot milk mixture over the yolk mixture, stirring to combine.

Return the egg and milk mixture to the cleaned saucepan and stir over low heat just until thickened (it should be 83°C on a sugar thermometer). Pass the mixture through a fine sieve into a bowl on ice. Stir in the Armagnac and 150 g of the date purée. Churn the mixture in an ice-cream machine, then transfer to an airtight container and freeze for 1 hour before serving. (Any leftover date purée can be stored in the fridge in an airtight container for 7 days, and served with vanilla ice-cream as a quick and delicious dessert.)

For the roasted pears, peel, quarter and core the pears, dropping each one into a large bowl of water with a good squeeze of lemon juice as you go, to prevent browning. Combine the sugar and water in a wide, heavy-based saucepan over medium–low heat. Cook for 5 minutes, until the sugar dissolves and the mixture becomes a dark amber caramel.

Add the pears and cook over medium–high heat for about 4-6 minutes on each side, depending on ripeness – there should be a slight resistance when poking them with a skewer. When ready, turn off the heat. To flambé, add the Armagnac and carefully use a long match to light the alcohol, standing well clear. It will flame up, then burn down and go out. Once the flames have subsided, lift the pears out of the caramel. They should be glazed in a delicious sticky syrup.

Serve the pears warm or cold (they are delicious either way) with scoops of Armagnac and date ice-cream.

CHEF'S NOTE

Ice-cream bases are always better when you make them the day before. We in the industry call this 'maturing'. When flambéing, make sure the area around the pan is uncluttered and there is no chance of anything else catching fire. To extinguish flames if necessary, cover completely with a large metal saucepan lid to cut off oxygen to the flame.

TO DRINK

The flavours of this dessert are encapsulated in a glass of tokaji aszu from Hungary. This rich and intense wine is made from botrytised grapes mixed with fresh grapes to create one of the most compelling sweet wines. Look for the sweeter styles labelled by a 'puttonyos' number greater than 4 to pair with this rich dessert. Aged examples are often the best when dates and Armagnac are involved.

MARKET TIP

I recently went on a trip to the Middle East and tasted some of the most amazing dates in the world. Try to find medjool dates if you can: they have a caramel, almost nutty chewy texture, and really are the kings of the Arabias!

Yeasted Buttermilk and Passionfruit Curd Doughnuts

Sour . Sweet . Texture

SERVES 8–10

VANILLA CITRUS SUGAR
3 citrus fruits of your choice
150 g caster sugar
1 vanilla bean, split,
 seeds scraped

PASSIONFRUIT CURD
250 ml strained passionfruit
 juice (preferably fresh,
 but tinned works fine)
5 eggs
210 g caster sugar
160 g soft unsalted butter

YEASTED BUTTERMILK DOUGHNUTS
30 g dried yeast
small pinch of sugar
75 ml lukewarm water
375 ml buttermilk
75 g unsalted butter, chopped
1 egg
650 g bread flour
75 g caster sugar
3 g salt
grapeseed oil, to deep-fry

Who doesn't love a doughnut? Fried batter in a vanilla sugar: yes please! The passionfruit cuts through the fattiness of the fried dumpling, and the yeasted buttermilk adds another dimension.

To make the vanilla citrus sugar, preheat the oven to 80°C. Remove the citrus peel in thin strips (avoiding the white pith) and spread out on a baking tray. Place into the oven for about 2 hours, until dehydrated.

Place the dried peel, sugar and vanilla seeds in a blender and blend on high until smooth. Store in an airtight container, and when ready to use spread onto a large plate.

For the passionfruit curd, put all the ingredients into a blender and blitz for 10–20 seconds. Transfer to a saucepan and cook, stirring, over medium heat for about 10 minutes until thick and creamy. It is okay if it boils as the eggs need to cook. Pass through a fine sieve and spread out on a flat tray. Cover the surface with plastic film. Leave in the fridge to cool completely. Once cooled, place in a piping bag fitted with a 2 cm plain nozzle and keep in the fridge until needed.

To make the doughnuts, whisk the yeast and sugar in a small bowl with the lukewarm water. Set aside for 3–4 minutes for the yeast to become active (it will start to froth). Heat the buttermilk and butter in a small saucepan over low heat until the butter has melted. Do not boil or the buttermilk will separate.

Place the egg, yeast mixture and buttermilk mixture in a large mixing bowl, or a stand mixer fitted with a dough hook, and sift in the flour and sugar. Mix until combined, then knead, in the mixer or by hand on a well-floured bench, for 4–5 minutes until the dough looks smooth and elastic. Be careful not to overwork the dough as it will stretch the gluten and result in 'hard' doughnuts.

Set the dough aside in the bowl, covered with plastic film, in a warm place for 30–45 minutes or until doubled in size. 'Knock back' the dough by picking it up and hitting it down. Roll the dough into a sausage shape and cut into 24 even portions. Roll into balls and put on a large greased baking tray, making sure to leave a 2 cm gap between each ball as they will expand. Leave to prove for a further 20 minutes.

Pour enough oil into a large deep saucepan so it is just under half full, and heat to 160°C. Using a slotted spoon or spatula slice under a doughnut and lift into the oil carefully. You should be able to cook in batches of four. Cook for 2 minutes on one side, then flip and cook for a further 1 minute, until golden brown. Remove with a slotted spoon and drain on paper towel.

Once the doughnuts are totally dry and free from any grease, roll in the citrus sugar to coat lightly. Pierce the side of each doughnut with the piping nozzle and pipe the passionfruit curd into the centre. Serve warm.

CHEF'S NOTE
You can make the doughnuts a little ahead of time, but just don't fill them with the curd too early otherwise they will go soft and mushy. If you need to warm them, bake them again briefly in the oven then fill with curd just before serving.

TO DRINK
Choose a New World late-harvest style for this dish. Late-harvest New Zealand sauvignon blanc would match the flavours with the sweet feeling on the palate mirroring the curd texture. Most of the production of these wines is in the Marlborough Valley.

MARKET TIP
Try to use old, wrinkly passionfruit whenever you can – they are normally sweeter, yet still contain a nice amount of acid. Look for plain flour labelled 'bread' flour at the supermarket – it contains more protein, which produces more gluten, essential for an elastic dough.

Autumn Heroes

Mushrooms.

    I love mushroom soup. Whether it's made from the bountiful button mushroom or its extravagant cousin, the pine – together with some good chicken stock, lashings of cream and a generous pinch of salt and pepper – when puréed to a velvety luxuriousness that coats the tongue, mushroom soup really is unbeatable on a crisp autumn day. It's such a versatile vegetable and I enjoy using it roasted, puréed, sautéed, pickled or finely shaved and raw. It's an endlessly interesting ingredient with a texture that's sometimes slippery and other times crunchy, and you can always rely on mushrooms to impart a deep earthiness to a dish. Mushrooms, thyme and garlic, a big spoon of foaming butter, some salt and pepper and you pretty much have a marriage made in heaven. Great with beef, firm flesh fish or as a brekkie treat, don't be shy to explore the magic of funghi.

Pears.

    The humble pear is another autumn favourite, and thinking about it as more than just a poached fruit or an after-sport snack really allows you to explore its full potential. Chutneys are great, with raisins or fresh grapes, whereas pickled pears are a wonderful condiment with cheese and even cured meats. Alternatively, toss pears in a smoking hot pan with some sugar to caramelise them and serve with stronger game meats such as venison or kangaroo. As for desserts, a warm pear clafoutis or pudding is a treat, especially when served alongside some Armagnac or brandy to liven things up, and aromatic cinnamon, star anise and vanilla to harmonise the marriage of flavours.

Autumn Menu 1

STARTER

Salt-baked Beetroot, Macadamia, Purslane

(page 109)

MAIN

Grass-fed T-Bone, Creamed Kale, Black Garlic

(page 119)

SIDE

Curried Pumpkin Mash, Herb Salad

(page 130)

DESSERT

Warm Chocolate and Chestnut Puddings

(page 137)

Autumn Menu 2

STARTER

Gnocchi, Gorgonzola, Silverbeet

(page 114)

MAIN

Braised Rabbit, Apricot, Witlof

(page 122)

SIDE

Coal-roasted Cabbage, Buttermilk, Sumac

(page 126)

DESSERT

Poached Quince Clafoutis,
Honey Ice-cream, Honeycomb

(page 134)

Winter

When the cold weather arrives, I instantly feel the need to slow-cook something! My body cries out for rich, hearty fare, whether it be in the form of braised pork cheeks, beef bourguignon, lamb shoulder or shanks, maybe even some osso buco with loads of root vegetables.

A hearty bowl of pumpkin soup goes a long way to warm up my insides, and comfort food is the order of the day. I love the gentle simmer of a casserole bubbling away all weekend that fills the kitchen with sweet herby aromas. Patience is definitely a virtue at this time of year.

Brussels sprouts aplenty, parsnips, carrots, turnips and swedes: these veggies make the perfect pairing for a simmering pot of slow-cooked goodness.

It's time to feed my body what it is craving to keep me going through the colder bite of winter. A big tray of my wife Bec's lasagne is just the ticket after a weekend of footy games, wind and rain! Oysters are also at their peak in the cooler months, and, though we generally associate them with summer, that's not when they are crisp, salty and ready to be slurped, freshly shucked, from their shells.

Oysters, Sauce Mignonette

Salty . Sour . Sweet

WINTER

STARTER

SERVES DEPENDS
HOW MANY OYSTERS
YOU EACH EAT!

3–4 dozen oysters, unshucked
  (see Chef's Note)
250 ml good-quality
  red-wine vinegar
6 large golden shallots,
  finely diced
freshly ground black pepper

Sauce mignonette is a condiment that consists of vinegar, shallots and black pepper, a perfect accompaniment to freshly shucked oysters.

Scrub the oyster shells thoroughly. Lay on a tray flat-side up and keep refrigerated until required.

Close to serving time, combine the vinegar and shallots, and season with pepper.

When ready to serve, using an oyster shucker, carefully open the oyster. The best way is to slide the sharp point into the back of the oyster and prise the shell apart.

Discard the top half of the shell and arrange the oysters in the half shell on a platter. Spoon the mignonette sauce over each oyster.

CHEF'S NOTE

Some people prefer to shuck the oyster from the side, so about half way along the shell. If you are not comfortable shucking the oysters yourself, make sure you buy the freshest oysters possible from a reputable fishmonger.

TO DRINK

A crisp white wine here is the perfect companion to the oysters and the acidity of the dressing, not to forget the creamy texture of the mollusc. Riesling, sauvignon blanc, albariño, muscadet and picpoul are just a few examples. My personal pick here is champagne – I prefer it blanc de blanc (100% chardonnay) and brut. Alternatively, a dirty vodka martini is very enjoyable.

MARKET TIP

I like to use a high-quality red-wine vinegar for my sauce mignonette, and you should too! It's like wine: the better the quality, the better the flavour. Higher quality vinegar has a rounder, sweeter flavour that's not quite as sharp as inferior products.

Tiger Prawns, Kombu Butter

WINTER

STARTER

SERVES 4

1 large sheet kombu
grapeseed oil, for greasing
6 g long green chillies
500 g unsalted butter,
   at room temperature
finely grated zest of 1 lemon
sea salt
12 tiger prawns, peeled
   and deveined, tails on
2 lemons, halved crossways

Fresh tiger prawns are so tasty in and of themselves, but I love to put an umami-packed compound butter with them to really enhance their natural flavour. Served simply with a good squeeze of lemon, a pinch of salt and some heat from the chillies in the butter, they don't need anything else.

Soak the kombu in a bowl of water for a couple of hours, until soft. Drain well, then finely chop.

Preheat the oven to 220°C. Lightly oil a baking tray and arrange the chillies on it in a single layer. Roast for 10–12 minutes, until well charred. Set aside to cool, then remove the seeds and chop the flesh.

Mix the butter, kombu, lemon zest and chopped chilli together until evenly combined. Season with sea salt.

Thread each prawn onto a bamboo skewer. Heat a chargrill pan over high heat. Cook the lemons cut-side down for a couple of minutes, until charred. Set aside. Cook the prawns on the grill for 2–3 minutes each side, until just cooked through and lightly charred.

Serve the prawns dressed with kombu butter, and with the charred lemons to squeeze over.

CHEF'S NOTE

Any leftover kombu butter will keep really well in the freezer. Roll it into ballotines or logs in plastic film and freeze to use another day.

TO DRINK

With the kombu giving extra savoury notes to the dish, I would drink a white wine from the Spanish coast – Rias Baixas in Galicia – made predominantly with 100% albariño, resulting in an intense bouquet, lean palate and beautiful volume for the butter. If possible, choose a wine sourced from the Val do Salnes sub-region as these are usually the fresher wines.

MARKET TIP

Kombu really is the king of seaweeds. Don't skimp on the quality you purchase. Look for it in Asian grocery shops or good health food shops.

Quail, Chestnuts, Golden Raisins

WINTER

STARTER

SERVES 4

2 tablespoons olive oil
4 quails, butterflied, backbones
    and wing tips reserved
200 g golden shallots, sliced
6 black peppercorns
1 bunch thyme
100 ml chardonnay vinegar
750 ml sweet white wine
500 ml brown chicken stock
sea salt
freshly ground black pepper
200 g golden raisins
100 g chestnuts, cooked
    and peeled
50 g butter
⅓ cup extra virgin olive oil

Chestnuts and grapes are a great combination, but here I have used golden raisins to replace the grapes. Their sweet and intense flavour is a perfect foil for the light gamey flavours of the quail and pairs perfectly with the chestnuts, too.

Heat the olive oil in a heavy-based saucepan over medium heat. Cook the quail backbones and wing tips for 10–12 minutes, stirring occasionally, until golden. Transfer to a plate and set aside.

Add the shallot to the pan and cook for a few minutes, until soft but not coloured. Add the peppercorns and thyme sprigs, then return the quail bones and trimmings. Stir in the vinegar and cook until reduced by half. Add the white wine and cook until reduced by two-thirds.

Heat the brown chicken stock in a separate saucepan. Add to the quail bone mixture. Bring to a simmer and cook over very low heat for 2 hours, skimming constantly, until reduced by half.

Remove the sauce from the heat and rest for 15 minutes, then pass through a fine sieve. Season to taste.

Meanwhile, soak the golden raisins in warm water for 25 minutes. Drain well. Cut the chestnuts into 8 pieces each. Foam the butter in a frying pan over medium heat and add the chestnuts. Cook until golden brown. Drain from the butter and combine in a bowl with the golden raisins and ¼ cup of the extra virgin olive oil. Set aside.

Preheat a cast-iron frying pan or chargrill pan over high heat. Drizzle the quail with the remaining extra virgin olive oil and season well with salt. Place breast-side down in the pan and cook for 2 minutes. Turn and cook the other side for 2 minutes. Remove from the pan and rest for 3 minutes. Return the quail to the pan and cook for a further 3 minutes each side. Set aside to rest for 5 minutes.

Meanwhile, reheat the sauce. Carve the quail, or leave whole if you prefer. Place on serving plates and arrange the chestnut and golden raisin salad on top of the quail. Spoon the warmed sauce over and around to serve.

CHEF'S NOTE

If you are not confident in de-boning the quail, you can always roast the birds whole and serve them on the bone. It's a little bit messier to eat, but a whole lot more fun! That said, I'm sure if you ask your butcher they will butterfly or spatchcock your bird for you – this just means flattening it out so it cooks a bit more quickly.

TO DRINK

The delicate white meat flesh from the quail, the dry fruit and the golden raisin call for a light red, ripe and complex with subtle texture, such as a pinot noir from Central Otago, New Zealand. The fruitiness of the wine gently accompanies the quail while the traditional light leathery notes from the sub-region of the Cromwell Basin complete the chestnut and golden raisin.

MARKET TIP

If you are cooking this dish outside of winter and have access to new season grapes, don't be scared to substitute and mix it up a bit. Red or white, doesn't matter. You could also add some celery or celeriac to this combo as well.

Pork and Duck Terrine, Carrot and Ginger Chutney

Spicy . Salty . Sweet . Texture

SERVES 10–12

CARROT AND GINGER CHUTNEY

3 carrots, finely grated
2 golden shallots, finely sliced
2 cm piece ginger, finely grated
200 ml apple cider vinegar
150 g brown sugar
finely grated zest and juice
    of 1 orange
pinch of saffron
200 ml water

MARINADE

150 ml white wine
¼ cup madeira
30 ml brandy
30 g salt
20 g sugar
pinch of quatre épices
1 carrot, coarsely chopped
2 cloves garlic, smashed
1 onion, quartered
2 sprigs thyme
1 bay leaf
freshly ground black pepper

TERRINE

700 g pork neck
400 g duck leg meat
150 g duck breast
250 ml duck or chicken stock
1 egg
50 ml cream
50 g pistachios, blanched,
    peeled and roughly chopped
sea salt
freshly ground black pepper
10 rashers thinly sliced belly (or
    streaky) bacon, or pancetta

toasted baguette, to serve

This is an oldie but a goodie! I can't claim this recipe as my own, as it was shared with me when I worked at Restaurant Paul Bocuse in Lyon, under Philippe Mouchel. It's just perfect!

To make the chutney, combine all the ingredients in a heavy-based saucepan. Bring to the boil over medium heat, stirring to ensure it doesn't catch on the bottom. Reduce the heat to very low and simmer gently for 45–60 minutes or until the liquid has evaporated and the mixture is thick. Place in a warm sterilised jar and refrigerate.

For the marinade, combine all the ingredients in a glass or ceramic dish and season with pepper.

To prepare the terrine, cut the pork, duck and veal into large cubes and add to the marinade. Mix well, then cover and refrigerate for 24 hours.

Remove the meat from the marinade, making sure the vegetables and herbs are left behind. Using a coarse blade on a mincer, mince the meat into a bowl standing over a bowl of ice. It's important to keep the meat mixture as cold as possible at this stage. Take out one-third of the mixture and mince it again, so that it has a slightly finer texture than the rest. This will help to bind the mixture. Return the minced meat to the fridge or freezer and drop the temperature to 2–4°C. Place the stock in a saucepan and simmer over medium heat until reduced by two-thirds. Transfer to a bowl and store in the fridge to chill.

Preheat the oven to 160°C. When the mince is very cold, transfer to the bowl of an electric stand mixer, and using the paddle attachment mix in the duck stock, egg, cream and pistachios.

To check for seasoning, cook a little 'tester', that is, take a small amount of the mixture and make a little patty. Cook in a frying pan, then taste to check the flavour. Season the remaining mixture accordingly.

Line a 2 litre capacity terrine mould with thinly sliced bacon or pancetta, hanging about 3 cm over each side. Fill with the mince mixture, pressing firmly. Fold the overhanging bacon back over the filling. Cover the terrine with baking paper then seal with foil or, if your mould has one, a lid.

Stand the terrine mould in a roasting pan and pour in enough water to come halfway up the sides. Bake for 50–60 minutes, turning the tray halfway through, until a meat thermometer shows 74°C when inserted into the centre of the terrine.

Remove the terrine from the oven and set aside to cool in the pan. When cool, take the terrine from the pan and place on a rimmed tray. Place a heavy weight on top of the terrine to compact the filling, and chill in the fridge overnight.

When cold, remove the terrine from the mould and using a hot knife cut into 2–3 cm thick slices. Serve with chutney and toasted baguette.

CHEF'S NOTE

Terrines are quite an involved process, but the time and effort is worth the end result and practice makes perfect. Quatre épices is considered the French allspice, usually with a peppery kick.

TO DRINK

Choose a rich and aromatic white wine here. A viognier with opulent notes and rich flesh will support the dish with its intense and delicate flavours while the dryness won't cover the delicious savoury meaty flavours. Alternatively, a pale ale is another nice choice. The hoppy flavour will balance the sweet carrots and intense ginger, while the malty character will bring structure for the terrine.

MARKET TIP

This dish is all about process and technique. With this, comes the flavour. Take your time to marinate the meat, mince it over ice, season, do a little tester, cook it gently and press overnight, then slice when cold. Patience is a virtue with this one!

Pumpkin Soup, Nutmeg Chantilly

Sweet . Spicy . Texture

SERVES 8–10

2 large butternut pumpkins
2 cloves garlic, smashed
5 sprigs thyme
olive oil, to drizzle
sea salt
freshly ground black pepper
1 litre chicken stock
1 litre double cream
1 litre milk

NUTMEG CHANTILLY
500 ml double cream
nutmeg, to season (preferably
   freshly grated)

My mum used to make pumpkin soup for us as kids, and I still love it today. Thick, rich and a little creamy, there's nothing better on a cold winter's night!

Preheat the oven to 180°C. Cut the pumpkins in half lengthways and scoop out the seeds and membrane. Place cut-side up on a large baking tray and top with garlic and thyme. Drizzle with olive oil and season with salt and pepper. Bake for 1 hour or until tender.

Combine the stock, cream and milk in a large saucepan. Bring to a simmer over medium–low heat and cook until reduced by half.

To make the nutmeg chantilly, season the cream with nutmeg and salt to taste, and whip to soft peaks. Cover and refrigerate until needed.

Scoop the tender flesh from the pumpkin skins and into a blender. Blend on high speed, until puréed. Add the stock mixture until the desired consistency. Reheat in a saucepan.

To serve, ladle soup into bowls and drop a small amount of nutmeg chantilly cream on top.

CHEF'S NOTE

This is our base recipe for most veloutés or soups: equal amounts of stock, dairy and the major ingredient (i.e. pumpkin, carrot, cauliflower etc). It's all based around the 1:1:1 ratio, a good base recipe for most soups.

TO DRINK

I always find a dry sherry with intense flavours comforting on those cooler winter days. To complement the pumpkin and nutmeg flavours, try the the nuttiness of a madeira, from the Portuguese island situated off the north-west coast of Africa. Its sweet texture is the perfect backdrop for this dish. Direct your choice toward a sercial, the driest style.

MARKET TIP

Different pumpkins have different uses so as with potatoes, for best results make sure you use the right veggie for the right job! Butternut is very versatile and good for most jobs, Queensland blue is great for scones, and golden nugget is a cracker for roasting in chunks with the skin on.

Osso Buco, Risotto Milanese

WINTER

MAIN

SERVES 4

OSSO BUCO
1 kg ripe tomatoes
4 × 350–450 g slices veal
    osso buco
¼ cup olive oil
2 cloves garlic, finely sliced
2 brown onions, diced
2 anchovies, chopped
250 ml dry white wine
2 litres veal or chicken stock
1 large sprig thyme
1 large sprig rosemary
1 large sprig sage
1 bay leaf
good pinch of saffron

GREMOLATA
½ bunch flat-leaf parsley,
    leaves picked and chopped
finely grated zest of 2 lemons
1 garlic clove, finely grated

RISOTTO
50 ml olive oil
5 golden shallots, finely diced
2 cloves garlic, crushed
500 g canaroli or arborio rice
pinch of saffron
50 g parmesan, grated
25 g butter
2 tablespoons olive oil
½ lemon (optional)
sea salt
freshly ground black pepper

One of the most famous dishes from Milan, the key ingredient in this risotto (aside from the rice) is saffron. Traditionally bone marrow is stirred back into it to make it glossy. It's a perfect foil for the slow-cooked veal, and a hearty winter night's feast. The classic way to serve this is to scatter it with the gremolata, which adds a wonderful freshness to the dish: the garlic, parsley and lemon work brilliantly with the tomato, meat and saffron.

For the osso buco, score a cross in the base of each tomato and place into a large heatproof bowl. Cover with boiling water and stand for 2 minutes, then drain. When cool enough to handle, slip off the skins. Cut in half crossways and scoop out the seeds, then roughly chop the flesh.

Season the meat well on both sides with salt and pepper. Heat 2 tablespoons of the olive oil in a large flameproof casserole over high heat. Sear the meat on both sides until well browned, then set aside. Reduce heat to low and heat the remaining olive oil. Add the garlic to the pan and cook until caramelised, then add the onion and anchovies and cook until tender.

Add the tomato to the pan and increase the heat to medium. Cook, stirring often, until the tomatoes have softened and broken down. Pour in the white wine and cook until reduced by two-thirds. Add the stock, herbs and saffron and bring to the boil.

Preheat the oven to 160°C. Return the meat to the pan and submerge in the liquid. Cover with a lid or foil and bake for 2–2½ hours, until the meat is just coming away from the bone. Allow the meat to rest in the cooking liquid until lukewarm, then transfer to a plate, cover and set aside. Strain the cooking liquid through a fine sieve, pressing on the vegetables to extract as much as possible. Place 1 litre of the stock in a saucepan for the risotto. Put the rest back into the casserole and return the meat. Reheat in a low oven while you make the risotto.

For the gremolata, mix the ingredients in a bowl and set aside.

To make the risotto, heat the reserved stock over medium–low heat and keep warm. Heat the olive oil in a wide saucepan over medium heat. Add the shallot and garlic and cook until tender. Add the rice and toast until lightly browned, then stir in the saffron. Add the hot stock a ladle at a time, stirring constantly and making sure it is fully incorporated before adding more. It will take about 25 minutes to cook the rice, adding stock and stirring, until it is creamy but the grains still have a slight bite. Stir the parmesan and butter into the risotto, with the olive oil and a squeeze of lemon juice if you like. Season to taste.

Serve the osso buco with the risotto, scattered with gremolata.

CHEF'S NOTE

Risotto, risotto, risotto . . . ah, how I love thee! There is a lot of dispute and discussion about how to cook the rice: some stir, some let it be, some even bake it in the oven. Ask most Italians and they all have their own little tricks depending on the region they are from. For me, I like to cook, add stock, and stir, add stock and stir. It gives the rice a rich, creamy texture.

TO DRINK

For this generous dish with lots of flavours, my pick would be a nebbiolo. With its thin texture and firm tannins, it gives a good energy to the match. A wine with a bit of age would add to the savouriness and create a link between all the flavours present. Preferably choose one from its native region in Italy, Barolo – the east side of the appellation produces more approachable wines in their youth.

MARKET TIP

When slow-cooking or braising meat, it's always best to let it cool in the juices before removing it from the pan. Doing so keeps the meat moist and this way any juices it releases will be soaked back into the meat, plus the remainder will make a great base for stocks and sauces.

Rib of Beef, Horseradish
Cream, Yorkies

Umami . Spicy . Texture

WINTER

MAIN

SERVES 4-6

1 × 2.2 kg beef rib roast
100 ml olive oil
sea salt
freshly ground black pepper

YORKSHIRE PUDDINGS
150 g plain flour
sea salt
freshly ground black pepper
4 large eggs
350 ml milk
½ teaspoon salt
vegetable oil (or beef
    dripping if you have some)

HORSERADISH CREAM
100 g horseradish, finely grated
250 g Greek-style yoghurt
2 cloves garlic, finely grated
2 teaspoons salt
juice of 2 lemons
Tabasco (optional), to taste

What can be greater than roast beef, horseradish and Yorkshire puddings, the quintessential Sunday lunch? You could add a touch of horseradish to the Yorkshire batter for an extra kick, or even a little nugget of black pudding would work brilliantly. Some hot gravy would also be fantastic.

Preheat the oven to 240°C.

To make the Yorkshire pudding batter, place the flour in a mixing bowl, season with salt and pepper and make a well in the centre. Whisk the eggs and milk together and add to the flour gradually, stirring gently to make a smooth batter. Strain the mixture through a fine sieve and set aside in the fridge to rest.

Use kitchen string to tie the beef between the ribs to keep a nice shape. Rub with the olive oil and season generously with salt and pepper. Place the meat on a rack sitting in a roasting pan. Roast for 15 minutes, then reduce the temperature to 180°C and bake for a further 50 minutes for medium-rare, basting occasionally with the pan juices.

Towards the end of the cooking time, heat a medium muffin pan in the oven to get piping hot. Remove the meat from the oven and rest, covered with foil, for a good 30 minutes. Increase the oven temperature to 200°C.

Working quickly, add a touch of vegetable oil or beef dripping to the hot tins and add the Yorkshire batter. Bake for 20-25 minutes or until puffed and golden brown on both top and bottom.

For the horseradish cream, mix all the ingredients together and taste to make sure it has enough punch (it may need more horseradish) and seasoning.

Reheat the beef for 6-7 minutes before carving. Serve the beef with the Yorkshire puddings and the horseradish cream.

CHEF'S NOTE

The best yorkies go into a super-hot tray and puff quickly – but be very careful when placing the batter into the tins so you don't burn yourself, as the tray and oil are extremely hot.

TO DRINK

Shiraz: thanks to its typical juiciness, which suits the generosity of the dish, and also its traditional spiciness. A fairly young wine would be good for this dish to keep the primary flavours of the beverage playing with the intensity of the horseradish. You can visit an iconic region such as the Barossa Valley for the volume and ripe style, or go for a fresher option from a cooler climate.

MARKET TIP

It is important to source your beef well. Think about the flavour and texture you enjoy when eating beef: grass-fed will certainly give you more flavour but also more texture when eating, whereas grain-fed will produce a less textural piece of meat. Look for some marbling through the meat and, if you want to spoil yourself, source some dry-aged meat – the ageing process will add character and flavour.

Baby Barramundi, Fennel, Blood Orange

SERVES 4

4 × 250 g fillets baby
   barramundi
2 teaspoon fennel seeds
100 ml dry white wine
50 ml olive oil
sea salt
freshly ground black pepper

SALAD

3 teaspoons fennel seeds,
   toasted and crushed
3 blood oranges, segmented,
   de-seeded
½ head radicchio, leaves
   roughly torn
1 fennel bulb, finely shaved
   (fronds reserved)
1 banana shallot (or 2 golden
   shallots), finely sliced
   into rings
1 bunch basil, leaves picked
   (stalks reserved)
50 g pitted black
   olives (optional)

DRESSING

2 tablespoons red-wine vinegar
2 teaspoons brown sugar
finely grated zest of ½
   blood orange
juice of 1 blood orange
100 ml extra virgin olive oil
sea salt
freshly ground black pepper

Fennel is at its best in winter, and rather than roasting
or braising it, here I've decided to serve a really simple shaved
fennel salad with orange. The anise flavour of the fennel
is a great match for the salty baby barramundi, and the acid
and sweetness from the blood oranges completes the trilogy.

Preheat the oven to 200°C. Tear 4 large squares of foil, big enough
to wrap each fish fillet generously, and lay a fillet on each one. Take the
reserved fennel fronds and basil stalks from the salad ingredients, and
place on top of the fillets along with the fennel seeds. Splash with the
wine and oil, and season with salt and pepper.

   Wrap the fish in the foil, sealing tightly so no steam can escape.
Place onto baking trays and bake for 15–20 minutes. Check one to test
that it is cooled, then re-seal and set aside to rest.

   For the salad, mix all the ingredients in a large bowl.

   To make the dressing, combine the vinegar, sugar, zest and juice
in a bowl. Add the extra virgin olive oil slowly, whisking to combine.
If you have a few spare fennel fronds, chop these roughly and add
to the dressing. Season to taste. Toss the salad with half the dressing,
then taste, adjust salt and add more dressing if needed.

   Serve the fish with the salad.

CHEF'S NOTE

The best way to shave the fennel and
shallot finely is on a mandolin, but take
care: the blade is razor sharp! Always
use the guard to hold the vegetable.

TO DRINK

My choice here is a chardonnay
from north of Burgundy: chablis. This
appellation, with its famous limestone soil,
produces a mineral chardonnay that's lean
and slightly savoury, while the creaminess
of the grape variety will enhance the
delicate flesh of the barramundi.

MARKET TIP

Use the fennel fronds (tips) to garnish the
salad – they have a wonderful flavour and
look great either picked or chopped.

Grilled Garfish, Lemonade Fruit, Oregano

WINTER

MAIN

SERVES 4

8 × 200 g garfish, butterflied
olive oil, for brushing
sea salt
freshly ground black pepper

PRESERVED LEMONADE FRUIT
4 lemonade fruit
200 g sugar
145 g salt
450 ml water

INFUSED OIL
½ teaspoon white peppercorns
1 teaspoon star anise
1 teaspoon fennel seeds
1 teaspoon coriander seeds
500 ml olive oil
3 cloves garlic, crushed
4 bay leaves
1 sprig thyme
½ bunch tarragon stalks

DRESSING
2 tablespoons lemonade
    fruit juice
30 ml red-wine vinegar
45 g Dijon mustard
25 g golden shallots, sliced
90 ml infused oil
sea salt
freshly ground black pepper
2 tablespoons chopped chives
2 tablespoons chopped
    flat-leaf parsley leaves
2 tablespoons
    chopped tarragon
15 oregano leaves (optional),
    to garnish

Garfish is a wonderfully tasty fish, great simply cooked under the grill or on a hot barbecue plate: crispy skin and soft flesh and dressed with a zingy vinaigrette.

To preserve the lemonade fruit, cut the fruit into very fine slices (use a mandolin if you have one) and pick out the seeds. Place into a 500 ml heatproof jar. Combine the sugar, salt and water in a saucepan. Bring to the boil, whisking well to dissolve. Pour the hot brine over the fruit and let sit for 20 minutes. Cover and refrigerate for at least 16 hours prior to use. It seems like a long process but is well worth it.

For the infused oil, toast all the spices in a dry frying pan over medium heat for a few minutes, until fragrant. Combine with the other ingredients in a saucepan and gently heat until just warm. Transfer to a jar and keep somewhere warm to infuse. The oil will keep for up to a couple of weeks.

To make the dressing, mix the juice of the lemonade fruit with the vinegar, mustard, shallot and infused oil and season with salt and pepper.

Preheat an oven grill. Place the garfish on a baking tray skin-side up. Brush with olive oil and season generously with salt and pepper. Cook under the grill until the skin is lightly crispy and the flesh is cooked through. Brush with a little more oil.

Take 8 slices of the preserved lemonade fruit from the jar and pat dry with paper towel. Use a kitchen blow torch or place under a hot grill to scorch them. This will really pronounce the flavour and bring great depth and character to this simple dish.

Mix the chopped herbs into the dressing. Place the fish on serving plates, add the preserved lemonade fruit and dress liberally with the herbed dressing. Garnish with the oregano.

CHEF'S NOTE
If you are really pedantic you can pin bone the garfish fillets, but sometimes I just remove them as I'm eating . . . it's up to you.

TO DRINK
Grilled fish and citrus call for white wine from sunny climes. My pick here is a wine from Greece, specifically the island of Kefalonia, made from the grape variety robola. The chalky soil from Kefalonia brings the ocean breeze into your glass and is supported by stone fruit and crisp citrusy notes.

MARKET TIP
Lemonade fruit is found during the winter months. It has a mild flavour somewhere between a lemon and a mandarin and lends itself well to both sweet and savoury applications.

SERVES 6–8

¼ cup vegetable oil
5 cloves garlic, finely sliced
2 celery sticks, diced
2 onions, diced
1 carrot, diced
500 g pork mince
500 g veal mince
2 tablespoons tomato paste
1 × 400 g can chopped tomatoes
250 ml beef stock
125 ml dry red wine
¼ cup balsamic vinegar
sea salt
freshly ground black pepper
1 × 300 g packet lasagne sheets
200 g parmesan, grated

BECHAMEL
1.5 litres milk
1 onion, cut into wedges
1 clove garlic, peeled
2 bay leaves
½ teaspoon ground nutmeg
120 g butter, diced
120 g plain flour
3 teaspoons fine salt

My wife loves to make lasagna, it's her thing and we as a family love to eat it – so it is a win for all of us. And it's such a classic feel-good dish that I had to include it!

Heat the vegetable oil in a large heavy-based saucepan over medium-low heat. Add the garlic and cook gently until fragrant and lightly golden. Add the diced vegetables and cook for a few minutes, stirring occasionally, until tender but not coloured.

Increase the heat to medium, add the mince and cook until lightly browned, breaking up the lumps with a wooden spoon as it cooks. Add the tomato paste and cook, stirring, for 2 minutes. Add the tomato, stock, wine and vinegar. Season with salt and pepper. Bring to a simmer, reduce the heat to low and cook partially covered for 45–60 minutes, until the sauce is thick and rich. Check the seasoning again and set aside.

To make the béchamel, combine the milk, onion, garlic, bay leaves and nutmeg in a saucepan. Heat, without boiling, then set aside for the flavours to infuse.

Melt the butter in a separate saucepan over medium heat and add the flour. Cook, stirring, for 2 minutes. Strain the infused milk and add to the flour mixture a little at a time, stirring until smooth between each addition. Season to taste.

Preheat the oven to 180°C. Grease a 30 cm × 20 cm × 6 cm baking dish. Spread a layer of meat sauce over the base of the dish, followed by a layer of pasta sheets then béchamel and parmesan. Repeat these layers 3 more times, finishing with béchamel and parmesan on top.

Bake for 30–40 minutes, until the pasta is tender and the top is golden brown. Stand for 10 minutes before cutting into squares to serve.

CHEF'S NOTE

You can certainly make the pasta yourself; it is greatly rewarding and will reduce the cooking time a little. You could even flavour the dough with squid ink or spinach purée.

TO DRINK

For this iconic dish from Bologna, I would pick a regional match here and choose a sangiovese, a sangiovese di romagna if possible. The grape variety shows some great examples in the New World as well, for example in the King Valley in Victoria.

MARKET TIP

If you bottle or preserve your own tomatoes, then a fresh passata or *sugo* is a great replacement for the canned tomatoes. But good-quality tinned tomatoes are a good sauce base too.

Salad of Roasted Jerusalem Artichokes

WINTER

SIDE

SERVES 8

BASIL OIL
200 g grapeseed oil
100 g basil leaves, washed

JERUSALEM ARTICHOKE CHIPS
400 g Jerusalem artichokes,
  thoroughly cleaned
grapeseed oil, to deep-fry

ROASTED JERUSALEM ARTICHOKE SALAD
1 kg Jerusalem artichokes,
  thoroughly cleaned
80 g butter
3 whole cloves garlic, peeled
15 sprigs thyme
sea salt
8 eggs
100 ml white vinegar
50 g roasted hazelnuts, crushed
¼ cup basil leaves
¼ cup pea shoots

The different textures and cooking techniques of the artichoke make this a really interesting dish. While complex in some regards, the end result is worth the effort.

To make the basil oil, place the grapeseed oil in a blender, and turn to low speed. Slowly feed the basil leaves into the oil through the hole at the top of the blender. Once all the basil is in, turn the mixer up to high speed and blend until the oil is steaming, 1–2 minutes. Once the oil is steaming, tip it into a mixing bowl over a bowl of ice. Stir the oil until it cools, then refrigerate overnight.

In the morning, place a sieve across a mixing bowl and line the sieve with a coffee filter. Pour the oil into the coffee filter and leave to drip through – it will take a few hours. The result should be an oil that is rich in colour and with the flavour of basil.

To make the Jerusalem artichoke chips, cut the artichokes into very thin slices, 2–3 mm thick (use a mandolin or vegetable slicer if you have one). Pour enough grapeseed oil into a large, deep saucepan so it is just under half full, and heat to 180°C. Fry the artichoke slices batch by batch. Do not fry them all at once or the oil temperature will drop and the chips will not be crisp. Cook for a couple of minutes, until crisp and golden. Lift the artichoke chips out of the oil with a slotted spoon and put them straight onto a plate lined with paper towel to absorb the excess oil.

To make the salad, preheat the oven to 180°C. Place a large heatproof frying pan over a medium–high heat.

Slice the artichokes in half. Pour a 2–3 mm thick layer of grapeseed oil into the hot pan and gently heat; the oil should be shimmering but not smoking. Place the artichokes cut-side down in the pan and fry until golden brown. Be careful not to overcrowd the pan; it is better to do this in batches if necessary. Once all the artichokes have been coloured, remove the pan from the heat and allow to cool down. Return all the artichokes to the pan, add the butter, garlic and thyme and season with salt.

Place the artichokes in the oven and check every 10 minutes until they are tender all the way through. When ready, remove the garlic and thyme and toss the artichokes in the butter in the bottom of the pan.

To cook the eggs, combine the vinegar with 1.5 litres water in a large saucepan. Add a good pinch of salt and bring to the boil. Crack the eggs into separate small ramekins. Using a wooden spoon, stir the water to create a whirlpool. Working one at a time, carefully slide an egg into the pot, ensuring it is rotating around the pan, which gives a great shape. Cook for 2 minutes, remove with a slotted spoon and place in iced water to stop the cooking. When cold, remove from the water. Repeat with remaining eggs and set aside until required.

To serve, cover the bottom of a serving platter with crushed hazelnuts and place the roasted artichokes on top. Garnish with artichoke chips, basil leaves, pea shoots, basil oil and the eggs.

CHEF'S NOTE

When frying the chips, make sure the oil is at the right temperature. If it's too hot, they will colour too quickly and burn around the edges; too cool and they will take on the oil and become soggy.

MARKET TIP

Jerusalem artichokes are like potatoes in the sense that there are a lot of cracks and crevices for dirt to really embed itself. The best way to go about cleaning them is to take an unused sponge or scour pad and just give them a hard scrub in a bowl of cold water, followed by a rinse under the tap. Jerusalem artichokes are very hearty, so they can take a little bit of abuse.

SERVES 8

2 fennel bulbs
2 white onions
4 small red-skinned potatoes
6 baby carrots
1 golden nugget pumpkin
sea salt
2 litres grapeseed oil
3 baby fennel
1½ tablespoons thyme leaves,
   lightly chopped

BOUQUET GARNI

½ bunch flat-leaf parsley
¼ bunch thyme
3 bay leaves
1 bulb garlic, cloves peeled
2 tablespoons black
   peppercorns
1 tablespoon coriander seeds
5 cloves
¼ teaspoon dried chilli flakes

A confit, in its simplest form, is meat or vegetables slow-cooked in fat. Fat is flavour and that's just what we get with this dish! I've used grapeseed oil in this dish, so it's vegan-friendly. If you really want to add a depth of flavour, then confit the veggies in duck fat – it really is delicious! Feel free to add any other of your favourite veggies to this dish too. You can add or subtract as you see fit.

Preheat the oven to 160°C.

For the bouquet garni, lay out a square of cheesecloth about 40 cm × 30 cm. Place all of the ingredients in the centre, leaving about 10 cm on each side. Fold the sides of the cheesecloth over the aromatics and roll the bundle up into a tight log. Tie the bouquet garni securely with three pieces of kitchen string.

Cut the fronds from the fennel and discard, then peel any dull outer layers from the bulb to reveal an interior of bright white and green. Halve the fennel, then cut each half into quarters lengthways and slice out the core.

Peel the onions, cut in half lengthways and remove the core. Cut each half into quarters lengthways. Cut each potato into 8 wedges. Peel the carrots and cut diagonally into large bite-sized pieces. Peel the pumpkin and cut the flesh into large dice. Combine all the vegetables in a very large casserole dish. Season liberally with salt and toss everything together.

Add the bouquet garni and pour the grapeseed oil over, making sure everything is submerged. Place a lid on the casserole and bake for 1 hour or until the vegetables are tender when tested with a skewer. They may cook at different times, so if you think some are ready before the others, then take them out and set aside.

Meanwhile, cut the baby fennel into very fine slices (use a mandolin if you have one). Submerge the strips in a bowl of iced water and place into the fridge to become crisp. When nearly ready to serve, drain thoroughly.

Strain the vegetables through a metal colander set over a large bowl and set aside for a few minutes so most of the oil runs off. Transfer the confit vegetables to a serving bowl. Garnish with the crisp baby fennel and the thyme leaves.

CHEF'S NOTE

You'll need some clean muslin or cheesecloth for this recipe.

MARKET TIP

If you can't get a golden nugget pumpkin, use half a butternut pumpkin.

Pommes Boulangères, Lemon Thyme

SERVES 8-10

1.25 kg white onions
80 g butter, plus extra
   for greasing
2 star anise
800 ml chicken stock
200 ml pouring cream
100 ml dry white wine
100 g butter, chopped
5 sprigs lemon thyme
5 sprigs rosemary
1.25 kg waxy potatoes
   (such as desiree)
freshly ground black pepper
100 g parmesan, finely grated
lemon thyme leaves,
   to garnish (optional)

Pommes boulangères means the 'baker's potatoes'. It's said that this dish originates from when the baker was finishing his day's work: he would place the tray of potatoes in the oven as it cooled, and in a couple of hours (or later that night) he would have a beautifully slow-cooked potato dish for his dinner. Superb!

Halve the onions lengthways and peel them. Cut lengthways into very fine slices (about 2 mm thick). Melt the butter in a large, deep frying pan over medium heat and add the onion, star anise and a pinch of salt. Cook, stirring every 5 minutes, until the onion has wilted and released its liquid. Reduce the heat to low.

Cook the onion for 30–40 minutes, stirring every 10–15 minutes, until a very deep brown colour. The onion will stick to the bottom of the pan and brown underneath, so stir and scrape as this happens.

Season with a little more salt, pick out the star anise and transfer the onion to a bowl to cool. You can make this ahead of time and refrigerate, covered, for up to 3 days.

Preheat the oven to 160°C. Combine the stock, cream, wine and butter in a saucepan. Bring to the boil over medium heat, then reduce the heat to low and simmer until reduced by about half. Place the thyme and rosemary in a mixing bowl and strain the stock mixture over the herbs. Set aside to infuse.

Peel the potatoes and cut into very thin slices, about 2 mm thick (use a mandolin if you have one). Season generously with salt and pepper and toss so that they are evenly seasoned.

Grease the base and sides of a 30 cm × 20 cm baking dish or 8 small cast-iron cocotte pans 10 cm diameter × 8 cm deep with butter. Make a layer of potato over the base of the dish. Spread a small amount of the onion over the potato and then sprinkle with a little of the parmesan. Make another layer of potato, followed by more onion and then more parmesan. Continue layering the ingredients, finishing with a layer of potato on top.

Strain the remaining stock mixture and pour it carefully over the potato. Cover with foil and bake for 45–60 minutes or until the liquid has been absorbed and the potato is tender when pierced with a knife. Uncover and cook a further 10–15 minutes until golden brown on top. Set aside to rest for 15–20 minutes before serving. Garnish with a few thyme leaves, if you like.

CHEF'S NOTE

Spend the time to layer the potatoes carefully. You will get a much better result if they are even and constructed correctly.

MARKET TIP

Use a white onion here, as the flavour is not as strong as your normal run-of-the-mill brown onion. And the real flavour comes from the caramelisation of the onion, so cook it until it's a deep golden colour.

Baby Carrots, Pecorino, Sage

SERVES 6

1 tablespoon black
    peppercorns
5 bay leaves
1 bunch baby yellow carrots
1 bunch baby orange carrots
1 bunch baby purple carrots
120 g butter
9 sprigs thyme
sea salt

**SAGE AND CARROT
TOP CRISPS**

1 bunch sage, leaves picked
tops from 1 bunch baby
    carrots, trimmed
grapeseed oil, to deep-fry
sea salt

GLAZE

350 ml chicken stock
150 ml carrot juice
100 ml dry white wine
1 tablespoon sugar
2 golden shallots, finely chopped
100 g cold butter, chopped
sea salt
100 g roasted almonds, chopped
1 × 150 g piece pecorino

The sweetness of the carrot marries a treat with the sharp
saltiness of the pecorino, and the pungent sage gives this dish
a true herbaceous hit!

To make the crisps, wash and dry the sage and carrot tops. Pour enough
grapeseed oil into a medium saucepan so it is just under half full, and
heat to 180°C. Line two baking trays with paper towel.

Place the sage leaves in a small metal sieve and lower into the oil.
Cook for 30–60 seconds until crispy. Drain on the paper towel and
season with salt. Repeat with the carrot tops.

Preheat the oven to 150°C. Bring a large saucepan of salted water
to the boil and add the peppercorns and bay leaves. Trim the baby
carrots, leaving about 1 cm of green on the end. Using a clean scourer
and cold water, scrub away any grit, dirt or dark spots on the carrots,
focusing especially around the tops.

Divide each bunch of carrots in half – one batch will be blanched
and the other pan-roasted. Take the yellow carrots from one batch
and cook in the boiling water for 6–8 minutes, until just tender. Lift out,
drain and lay out on a baking tray. Repeat with the orange and then the
purple carrots. Keep them apart on the tray, as the colour from the purple
carrots will bleed into the orange and yellow.

Meanwhile, heat a frying pan over medium–high heat. Add one-third
of the butter with 3 sprigs of the thyme. Once the butter is foaming and
hot, add the yellow carrots. Toss them in the butter and season with
salt. Cook until brown, only moving them every 3–5 minutes. Once the
carrots are brown on all sides and al dente, transfer to another baking
tray. Repeat with the orange and then the purple carrots, adding more
butter and thyme for each batch.

For the glaze, combine the stock, juice, wine, sugar and shallot in
a large wide saucepan over medium heat. Bring to the boil, then add
the butter. Cook until reduced to a thick syrupy glaze.

Remove the glaze from the heat and season with salt. Add all the
carrots and almonds and toss everything together until well coated.
Transfer to a serving platter and garnish with the sage and carrot top
crisps, then finely grate the pecorino over the top.

CHEF'S NOTE

Sometimes I don't peel my baby carrots. Scrubbing them with
a clean, new scourer or brush keeps the nutrients in the skin
and the natural shape of the carrot too. This is a good way
to clean baby vegetables, as peeling often gives vegetables
an unattractive shape; this should leave you with a very clean
carrot that retains its original character and shape.

MARKET TIP

Try to use as many different kinds of heirloom carrot as you
can find for this dish – it's visually appealing and the contrast
of colours and flavours will be pleasantly surprising. Make sure
the tops are bright green and fresh looking – not wilted.

Glazed Parsnip, Golden Raisins, Pepitas

SERVES 6

100 g pepitas
sea salt
splash of olive oil
1 kg small parsnips, peeled
50 g butter
freshly ground sichuan
   pepper, to taste
850 ml chicken stock
5 juniper berries
5 star anise, coarsely crushed
3 bay leaves
50 ml honey
lemon juice, to taste
2 tablespoons chopped tarragon
¼ cup golden raisins

This dish calls for a little bit of technique that will elevate your roast parsnip to the next level. Glazing the parsnip will result in a deep, rich flavour and a gorgeous shine, while the pepitas add a glorious and satisfying crunch.

Preheat the oven to 160°C. To toast the pepitas, mix them with salt and a splash of olive oil, lay them out on a baking tray and bake in the oven for 10 minutes.

Cut each parsnip in half. Melt the butter in a frying pan over medium heat. Add the parsnips, season with salt and sichuan pepper and toss to coat. Add the chicken stock, juniper berries, star anise and bay leaves and bring to the boil. Cook until the liquid has almost completely evaporated. Add the honey and cook until the liquid has become rich and thick and the parsnips are glazed. Taste and season with salt and lemon juice, then add the tarragon and raisins. Transfer to a serving plate and garnish with the toasted pepitas.

CHEF'S NOTE

Glazing vegetables is a brilliant way to capture their natural sweetness and works well with carrots and onions, too. Maple syrup makes a good alternative to honey in this recipe.

MARKET TIP

Try to find some young baby parsnips if you can – they have a smaller core and are much sweeter than the larger ones.

Apple Tarte Tatin, Star Anise Ice-cream

Spicy . Sweet . Temperature

WINTER

DESSERT

SERVES 6–8

STAR ANISE ICE-CREAM
8 star anise
360 ml milk
35 g skim milk powder
750 ml cream
150 g egg yolks (about 7)
200 g caster sugar

APPLE TARTE TATIN
200 g caster sugar
100 g unsalted butter, chopped
4 large pink lady apples,
   peeled, quartered and cored
375 g butter puff pastry, thawed
icing sugar, to dust

One of my all-time favourite desserts, nothing beats the golden pastry and roasty, slightly tart apple flavour with a rich, dark caramel. Add a big scoop of spiced star anise ice-cream and it's winter's delight!

To make the ice-cream, preheat the oven to 180°C. Place the star anise on a baking tray and roast for 6 minutes, until fragrant. Combine the milk and star anise in a medium saucepan over medium heat. Add the milk powder and whisk until dissolved. Add the cream and bring just to the boil. Meanwhile, whisk the yolks and sugar together in a heatproof bowl until pale. Add one-third of the milk mixture to the yolk mixture and whisk to combine. Pour back into the pan with the remaining milk mixture. Stir over low heat until thickened (until a thermometer reaches 83°C). Pass through a fine sieve into a bowl. Stand the bowl in a larger bowl of ice and stir to release the heat. Once cooled churn in an ice-cream machine. Transfer to an airtight container and freeze.

For the apple tarte tatin, preheat the oven to 190°C. Divide the sugar between six to eight deep ovenproof frying pans, 13 cm in diameter, shaking to make an even layer across the base. (Alternatively you could use one large pan, 25 cm in diameter.) Place over medium heat and melt the sugar without stirring until it has caramelised to an amber colour. Divide the butter equally between the pans and mix until well combined. Set aside to cool slightly. Arrange the apple over the base of the pans, packing the pieces in as tightly as possible.

Cut rounds from the pastry 2 cm larger than the diameter of the frying pans. Place over the apple and tuck the excess pastry down inside the pans.

Place the pans in the oven and bake for 25 minutes, until the pastry is puffed and golden. Stand for 5 minutes, so the caramel can cool and thicken slightly, making it safer and easier to turn out. Place a serving plate that is larger than the diameter of the pan on top and quickly invert. Be very careful, as hot caramel may spill out. Lift the pans off the tartes and stand for 5 minutes before serving.

Serve each tarte with a generous scoop of ice-cream.

CHEF'S NOTE

Don't be scared to take your caramel nice and dark – the apples will absorb it, while also releasing their own juices, and it will become a little lighter once cooked. Just don't burn it!

TO DRINK

Confit apple and buttery puff pastry are a perfect match for a late-harvest chenin. This will bring a texture and flavour profile with amazing results. Choose one from the Margaret River in Western Australia. Or go for a pommeau de Normandie (apple juice fortified with apple brandy) or a French-style semi-sweet cider, which is the regional match for this dish.

MARKET TIP

Choose the right apple! Something like a pink lady that is firm, slightly acidic and cooks well without breaking down is my personal choice.

Molasses-roasted Pineapple, Frangipane, Vanilla Ice-cream

Sweet . Spicy . Temperature

WINTER

DESSERT

SERVES 4-6

VANILLA ICE-CREAM
750 ml milk
2 vanilla beans, split,
   seeds scraped
200 g caster sugar
35 g skim milk powder
360 ml cream

MOLASSES-ROASTED PINEAPPLE
8 cloves
2 star anise
2 cinnamon sticks
1 teaspoon whole pink
   peppercorns
1 fresh ripe pineapple, peeled,
   quartered lengthways and
   core removed
220 g molasses (or dark
   brown) sugar
1 teaspoon ground ginger
50 ml cold water
30 ml dark rum

FRANGIPANE
250 g unsalted butter, at room
   temperature, chopped
250 g caster sugar
4 eggs, at room temperature
250 g ground almonds
75 g rice flour

Frangipane is just a fancy name for almond cake, really! Roasted pineapple and rum syrup go together like strawberries and cream, and the frangipane soaks up all the rum and molasses goodness . . . it's an incredible combination that you just have to try.

To make the vanilla ice-cream, combine the milk, vanilla beans and seeds in a medium saucepan. Add the sugar and milk powder and place over medium heat. Whisk continuously until the sugar and milk powder have dissolved. Stir in the cream and bring back to the boil. Remove from the heat and strain through a fine sieve into a bowl. Stand the bowl in a larger bowl of ice and stir to release the heat. Once cooled, churn in an ice-cream machine. Transfer to an airtight container and freeze.

To roast the pineapple, preheat the oven to 190°C. Place the whole spices into a baking dish and toast in the oven for 6 minutes or until fragrant.

Place the pineapple into a large non-stick ovenproof frying pan. Sprinkle the molasses sugar and ginger evenly over the pineapple and add the toasted spices and cold water. Cook gently over medium heat for 10 minutes. Transfer to the oven for a further 10 minutes, glazing the pineapple twice during roasting by spooning the melted sugar back over the fruit. Remove from the oven and sprinkle with rum. Leave to cool. Remove the pineapple from the pan and cut the quarters in half so you have 8 pieces, then cut those into smaller chunks. Set aside. Add a dash of water to the syrup in the pan and stir over medium heat until smooth. Strain and set aside for serving.

For the frangipane, preheat the oven to 165°C and line a 22 cm diameter round cake tin with baking paper. Use an electric mixer to beat the butter and sugar together on high until soft and creamy. Add the eggs one at time, beating until combined after each addition. Mix the ground almonds and rice flour together, then, with the mixer on low speed, add gradually until incorporated.

Arrange the chunks of pineapple in an even layer in the bottom of the prepared tin. Spoon the frangipane on top of the pineapple and spread out evenly. Refrigerate for 20 minutes. Bake for 35–40 minutes or until golden and a skewer inserted into the centre of the cake comes out clean. Remove from the oven and allow to cool slightly. Turn out onto a serving plate with the roasted pineapple on the top.

To serve, cut the warm cake into portions and place on serving plates. Top with a generous scoop of vanilla ice-cream and drizzle with the reserved spiced rum syrup.

CHEF'S NOTE

When cleaning the pineapple, be pretty brutal – make sure you remove any little spikes and all skin. Ensure you have an even natural shape too. If you want to make the cake ahead of time, simply reheat in the oven to serve.

TO DRINK

A fortified wine provides concentrated aromas that lend themselves to the pineapple and, due to its alcohol content, it will still shine alongside the cold ice-cream component of the dish. Perhaps a cognac or a Pineau des Charentes – the fruit flavours and spices make a perfect match.

MARKET TIP

Nothing beats fresh vanilla beans. The aroma, the fragrance and the flavour just don't compare to an essence. A little tip: make sure you split and scrape your vanilla beans so the beautiful little fleck of the seeds is apparent in the syrup.

Annie's Lemon Delicious

Sour . Sweet . Texture

SERVES 6

220 g caster sugar
90 g butter, at room
   temperature, plus extra
   for greasing
finely grated zest and juice
   of 2 limes
finely grated zest and juice
   of 1 lemon
3 eggs, separated
120 g self-raising flour
750 ml milk
pinch of salt
icing sugar, to dust
thick pure cream, to serve

Annie is the mother of Danny, my pastry chef. She came to me a few years ago and asked if I would take a young hooligan under my wing and train him. I like a challenge so I obliged. It's been great to watch him grow into a talented young man, and this is his favourite recipe for his favourite person: his mum. Thanks, Annie.

Preheat the oven to 180°C. Use electric beaters to beat the sugar, butter and citrus zest until pale and fluffy. Add the egg yolks one at a time, beating well after each addition. Add the flour and milk alternately in batches and beat well until a smooth batter forms. Add the citrus juices and beat until just combined.

In a separate bowl, use clean beaters to beat the egg white with a pinch of salt until stiff peaks form. Fold one-third of the egg whites through the batter to loosen it, then fold in the remaining egg white until just combined.

Pour the mixture into a well-buttered ceramic oven dish (30 cm long × 15 cm wide x 13 cm deep) and place in a deep roasting pan. Put into the oven and pour enough hot water into the roasting pan to come halfway up the sides of the dish. Bake for 35–40 minutes, until puffed and golden. Leave to stand for 10 minutes.

To serve, dust generously with icing sugar and serve with pure cream. Eat immediately.

CHEF'S NOTE

Teaching is such a fundamental part of life in the restaurant industry – I've had great teachers throughout my career and they've been very special people in my life. I love being in a position now where I can be mentoring up-and-coming young chefs. I learn new things along the way, too.

TO DRINK

The light texture and citrus flavours in this dessert sound like sparkling wine to me. There are amazing examples of this produced all around the world but if you prefer a bit of sweetness to pair with it, choose a champagne demi sec or an amiable Italian style. My personal choice is a cava. This dry Spanish sparkling wine is produced in the Catalonia region and is close to the non-vintage champagne style.

MARKET TIP

This recipe could be made with any other citrus, if you like – orange, more lime, or even grapefruit. Lemonade fruit or meyer lemons are a little bit special and will amaze your family or guests.

Australian Black Truffle Brie

SERVES 4

1 × 250 g wheel double
   or triple cream brie
1 × 10 g Australian black truffle
fruit bread or baguette,
   to serve

Being extravagant with black truffles when they are in season is one of life's more decadent pleasures. Shaving lashings of Aussie black truffle in between a ripe, rich brie or triple cream is truly a celebration of the season.

Take a length of kitchen string about 40 cm long. Wrap it around the outside of the wheel of brie, crossing it where the ends meet. Pull on the ends of the string so that they cut cleanly through the cheese horizontally.

Place the cheese halves on a piece of cheesecloth or baking paper. Shave the truffle onto the cut surfaces – use a truffle slicer if you have one.

Sandwich the cheese back together, wrap in the cloth or paper and refrigerate for 2–3 days. Once the truffle scent has permeated through the cheese it is ready to eat.

Return to room temperature, then serve the truffled cheese smeared on fruit bread or baguette.

CHEF'S NOTE

Don't be shy when using truffles. Keep the trim for sauces and mousses, and shave the big bad boys over risotto, risoni, scrambled eggs or handmade pasta. Creamy sauces are best.

TO DRINK

Old chardonnay from the Margaret River to marry the creaminess of the brie and the earthiness of the truffle.

MARKET TIP

Smell, smell, smell. That's the best way to choose both a great truffle and a cheese that's ripe and ready. Check the firmness of the cheese and ensure it's just a little ripe when using it in this dish.

Blood Orange and Campari Pots de Crème

WINTER

DESSERT

SERVES 8

BLOOD ORANGE AND CAMPARI MARMALADE
1.1 kg blood oranges
2 litres cold water
2 kg caster sugar
juice of 2 lemons
2 tablespoons Campari

VANILLA POTS DE CREME
750 ml cream
250 ml milk
1 vanilla bean, split, seeds scraped
10 egg yolks
220 g caster sugar
1 tablespoon demerara sugar

A one-pot wonder that, when ready, can be kept in the fridge for when guests arrive. Campari and blood orange are a match made in heaven, and the creaminess of the pots de crème makes this a sublime and special treat. These pair beautifully with my Yeasted Buttermilk and Passionfruit Curd Doughnuts (page 142), and while blood orange is especially magical, feel free to use whatever citrus fruit you like for this recipe.

To make the marmalade, thinly slice the oranges and discard the ends. Place in a large saucepan and add the water. Bring to the boil, reduce the heat to low and simmer very gently, covered, for 1½ hours or until the rind is soft.

Stir in the sugar and lemon juice. Increase the heat to medium and bring to the boil. Boil briskly for about 35 minutes, until the marmalade reaches setting point (108°C). To test, place a spoonful of mixture onto a chilled plate to cool. If the mixture wrinkles when pushed with a spoon, it is ready.

Turn off the heat and add the Campari. Allow the marmalade to cool for 5 minutes, then stir to distribute the fruit evenly. Transfer to twelve 250 ml capacity warm sterilised jars, filling to about 5 mm from the rim of the jar. Place the lids on tightly and stand the jars upside down for 2 minutes. Don't forget to turn them over again, or the gap will set at the bottom of the jar. The marmalade is ready to use as soon as it is cool and set, and will keep for several months in closed jars in the fridge.

For the pots de crème, preheat the oven to 150°C. Bring the cream, milk and vanilla bean and seeds to a simmer in a saucepan over medium heat. Meanwhile, whisk the yolks and caster sugar in a bowl until pale. Gradually add the cream mixture, whisking gently until incorporated. Put 1½ tablespoons of the blood orange marmalade into each of eight 250 ml capacity ovenproof ramekins. Pour the cream mixture over the marmalade.

Line a roasting pan with a folded tea towel. Place the ramekins on the tea towel. Cover the pan with foil, leaving one corner open. Place the pan into the oven and pour enough boiling water into the pan (through the open corner) to come halfway up the sides of the ramekins. Close the foil and bake for 50–55 minutes or until the custards are just slightly wobbly in the centre.

Lift the ramekins out of the water and leave to cool for 15 minutes. Transfer to the fridge to set for at least 6 hours, or overnight if possible.

To serve, take the pots de crème from the fridge. Sprinkle the surface of each with demerara sugar. Use a kitchen blow torch to caramelise the sugar to a dark amber colour. Leave to cool for 1 minute before serving.

CHEF'S NOTE

The marmalade can be kept in the fridge and used in the morning on your toast or crumpets.

TO DRINK

The citrusy bittersweet marmalade and the creamy texture call for an aromatic and fresh wine. An aromatic grape variety such as muscat has this profile. Make sure to choose a naturally sweet example, not a fortified one.

MARKET TIP

The blood orange season is short (and sweet) so when they are around, use them wherever possible. Jams, preserves, marmalades, pickles or juice, they are delightful!

Jerusalem artichokes.

Another one of the ugly but delicious tubers, Jerusalem artichokes are sadly a bit misunderstood. But unlock the nutty and earthy flavour profile within and you'll start a love affair with something delicious and sweet. Perfect for purées, sautéed or fried, boiled and crushed with butter and herbs, these little rippers will delight and astound. During preparation, be careful they don't oxidise and turn a nasty brown colour on the surface – make sure you either peel and place them in acidulated water (see Glossary), or use them immediately. When roasted whole and unpeeled, the light and fluffy inside is a perfect foil for the toasty notes of the caramelised skin. Winter days come alive with a wonderful artichoke soup, but this seasonal hero also marries well with hard cheeses, celeriac, potato and even pumpkin, too.

Citrus.

As I've outlined a number of times throughout this book, quite often simplicity is the key. The problem with that is there is nowhere to hide, and any imperfections become an obvious mistake. Enter the lemon or lime tart. When perfect, it's a thing of beauty and joy, the pastry so fine and crisp, the tangy filling providing a warm, jelly-like wobble. The abundance of citrus in winter makes these tarts a joy to cook and eat, but simmering copper pots of marmalades, curds, jams and chutneys also fill the house with a zesty tang. It's the flexibility of the citrus family that encourages its use, either sweet or savoury, with seafood, poultry, in desserts and puddings, preserves and conserves. And of course, these gems offer plentiful opportunities to explore wonderful pairings with a whole host of wines, too. Who ever said that winter was no fun?

Winter Menu I

STARTER

Pumpkin Soup, Nutmeg Chantilly

(page 159)

MAIN

Rib of Beef, Horseradish Cream, Yorkies

(page 162)

SIDES

Pommes Boulangères, Lemon Thyme

(page 173)

Baby Carrots, Pecorino, Sage

(page 174)

Glazed Parsnip, Golden Raisins, Pepitas

(page 177)

DESSERT

Apple Tarte Tatin, Star Anise Ice-cream

(page 178)

Winter Menu 2

STARTERS

Oysters, Sauce Mignonette

(page 152)

Tiger Prawns, Kombu Butter

(page 154)

MAIN

Baby Barramundi, Fennel, Blood Orange

(page 165)

DESSERT

Annie's Lemon Delicious

(page 183)

Glossary

Cooking terms

ACIDULATED WATER

Water that includes, for example, lemon juice. Used when preparing ingredients that tend to oxidise (turn brown) when cut, such as apples or Jerusalem artichokes.

BARIGOULE

A classic French cooking technique originating in the Provence region, normally used with artichokes that have been prepared and cooked with vegetables, white wine and white-wine vinegar.

BASTE

To moisten during cooking with fat or liquid to prevent an ingredient drying out or to impart flavour or glaze.

BLANCH

A classic technique of cooking vegetables in boiling, salted water until al dente before plunging into iced water to prevent further cooking. This keeps the required doneness until required, and helps maintain colour and texture.

BRAISE

To cook something at a low temperature in liquid/stock until meltingly tender. It's great to braise on the bone if using meat.

BRULEE

To caramelise with a blow torch to create a thin, crispy layer. Imagine crème brûlée or brûléed figs with sugar.

CHAR

A way of cooking over flames that blackens the outside while imparting a smoky flavour.

CONFIT

To cook meat, fish or vegetables gently in fat or butter until meltingly tender, rich and delicious, the classic being duck confit.

CURE

The process of preserving food using combinations of salt, nitrates, sugar and citrus to draw moisture out and impart flavour.

EMULSIFY/EMULSION

To mix two ingredients that do not necessarily mix well together, such as oil and vinegar for a vinaigrette; hollandaise sauce is a classic emulsion of eggs and butter.

GIRELLO

The eye of the silverside, very lean and full of flavour, great for a pot roast.

GRADE

To put them into order, for example cooking things of similar size so they cook in the same time. Also grade for quality best to worst.

JOINTING

To follow the natural seams or bone structure of an animal to break it down. A perfect example is chicken broken down into breasts, wings, thighs and drumsticks.

JULIENNE

A knife cut, usually vegetables cut into long, very fine strips.

MACERATE

To use a liquid to soak or soften a product and to add flavour – think of cherries in kirsch or prunes in Armagnac.

MANDOLIN

A piece of equipment with an extremely sharp blade that enables cooks to slice super finely and evenly, creating a really consistent product.

MICROPLANE

A hand-held fine grater, very sharp and extremely useful.

QUENELLE

Making a quenelle is a way to give a beautiful oval shape using two spoons to an homogenous mass of food, examples being ice-cream, sorbet, beef tartare.

REDUCTION

To reduce a liquid such as a sauce or stock to intensify the flavour.

RENDER

To cook the fat out of meat.

RILLETTES

Similar to making a pâté, cooking something in fat or incorporating fat to create a rich paste. Pork is commonly used but rabbit or salmon are both fantastic.

SAUTE

To cook in a small amount of fat over high heat making sure the food does not stick to the pan, from the French word *sauter* ('to jump').

SCORE

To cut through the surface of an ingredient to enable heat and flavour to penetrate more easily during the cooking process.

SEAL OR SEAR

To caramelise pieces of fish or meat in a hot pan before finishing the cooking in the oven. This process creates a rich colour on the outside and generates a contrast in texture and flavour.

SWEAT

To cook something gently in a pan with a little oil or butter over low heat to soften and bring out the natural juices, normally at the start of the cooking process.

TRUSS

To tie a bird with kitchen string before cooking helps it cook more evenly as it makes a more even mass. If you don't truss the bird enough, hot air circulates through the open cavity and dries the breast meat out before the thigh and legs are cooked properly.

WATER BATH

A piece of equipment that allows us to cook at a constant temperature and gives an even cooking finish circulating liquid around the product. This can be achieved at home by placing a ceramic dish in a roasting pan filled with hot water.

00 FLOUR

Has a finer grain than plain flour resulting in light, airy bread and soft cakes, and is always used in pasta dough. The grading system (2, 1, 0 or 00) comes from Italy.

BALLOTINE

A boned chicken or duck leg, stuffed with forcemeat or mousse, tied and poached or roasted. Ballotine refers to the shape – *balle* meaning 'package' in French.

BOUQUET GARNI

A bundle of herbs tied with string that is added to stocks or soups to impart flavour but removed before serving. Usually consisting of thyme, parsley stalk, bay leaf, rosemary.

CHERVIL

A delicate herb with a gentle aniseed flavour. Sometimes called French parsley.

CUMQUAT

Small orange fruit that is part of the citrus family, with edible sweet rind and acid flesh, great for marmalade.

DRAGONCELLO

A delicious dressing originating in Tuscany, great with seafood, vegetables and poultry. Normally made using stale bread, olive oil, anchovies, red-wine vinegar, garlic and tarragon.

ESPELETTE

A variety of chilli that is produced in south-western France and is mildly hot. Used dried and ground as a seasoning.

FROND

The tips of a herb or leafy top of a vegetable (fennel, carrot). Also the shape of a herb as it shoots out from the stem.

LARDON

A chunk or cube of bacon.

LOVAGE

A pungent herb close to the parsley and celery families.

VERJUS

A highly acidic juice made by pressing unripe grapes, with a gentler flavour than vinegar. It is not fermented and is not alcoholic. Used in dressings.

WITLOF

Part of the chicory family, moderately bitter, great in salad but also braised.

Acknowledgements

A lot of hard work goes into making a cookbook happen, that's for sure: writing, researching, ordering, preparing, taking photos, designing . . . So many people contribute to make this dream a reality, and I'd like to take a moment just to say thank you.

To Izzy and the team at Penguin Random House, a big thanks for believing in my idea and helping me to meet my deadlines . . . sometimes! Your patience and support really have been amazing.

To the kitchen team that helped get this over the line, from the food shots to helping with recipes: a big shout out to Valentin Barrère, Danny Rahilly, Stuart McVeigh, Michael Gellinas, Xavier Le Roy, Quentin Gallouedec and Stevie Nairn. Thank you also to Fabien Moalic, my amazing sommelier, for all your input on the drink pairings.

To the office team at Pickett & Co, Kim Berkers and Brittany Bordignon, who help me with practical things like formatting, plus my outside commitments and organising my life.

For making the recipes and the food look so bloody tasty and delicious, thank you to photographer Dean Cambray and stylist Leesa O'Reilly. This is two in a row now, and the results are amazing – again.

To Tracy Rutherford, for all your careful editorial work, and to Evi O. Studio, for creating such a beautiful design for the book. Thank you both.

To my old mate from the UK, TPB, for writing such a beautiful foreword and just listening to me talk about the concept and ideas. Cheers, buddy.

To the entire team that works in the restaurants and behind the scenes: at Estelle, Saint Crispin, Matilda and Pickett's Deli. Without so many wonderful people behind me helping me live my dream, I wouldn't be able to achieve things such as this.

To my mum, Andrea, my father, Jim, and my brother, Luke: thanks for putting up with me for so many years and supporting me when times have been good and bad. Big love.

Last but not least by any stretch of the imagination, a massive thanks to my biggest supporter: my wife, Bec. It's your hard work, support and all the time you spend looking after our three beautiful children, Harrison, Matilda and Oscar (and me!), that allows me to do what I do, day in, day out. Love you, sweetheart.

Recommended Suppliers

FRESH GENERATION

fresh fruit and vegetables
Gerry Katiforis
03 9687 9225
www.freshgeneration.com

FRIEND AND BURRELL

fresh truffles, caviar and Spanish jamón
Simon Friend
04 0542 4860
www.friendandburrell.com.au

GAMEKEEPERS

quality meats, game and small goods
Jerome Hoban
03 9555 7000
www.gamekeepersmeat.com.au

GLENORA HERITAGE PRODUCE

fresh fruit and vegetables
Andrew Wood
03 5433 5396
glenoraheritageproduce@optusnet.com.au

MILAWA CHICKEN

free-range poultry
Russell Mickle
04 2857 0492
russell@milawafreerangepoultry.com.au

SPURRELL FORAGING

fresh foraged herbs and plants
Liam Spurrell
04 1903 1423
liam@spurellforaging.com.au

OCEAN MADE SEAFOOD

fresh seafood
George Lucas
03 9486 0399
www.oceanmade.com.au

SHER WAGYU

wagyu beef from Ballan, Victoria
Vicky and Nick Sher
03 5368 2345
www.beefcorp.com.au

VIC'S PREMIUM QUALITY MEAT

premium quality meat
Ben Gisonda
03 9368 9368
www.vicsmeat.com.au

CAMPANIA ALIMENTARI

dry goods
Robert Iannantuono
04 0985 5500
www.campania.com.au

ST DAVID DAIRY

dairy products
03 9415 7732
www.stdavid.com.au

INSPIRED INGREDIENTS

innovative ingredients
Rodd Blutman
04 0335 8922
rodd@inspiredingredients.com.au

Index

LANTERN

UK | USA | Canada | Ireland | Australia
India | New Zealand | South Africa | China

Lantern is part of the Penguin Random House group
of companies whose addresses can be found at global.
penguinrandomhouse.com.

First published by Lantern, an imprint
of Penguin Random House Australia Pty Ltd 2019

Cover and text design by Evi O. Studio © Penguin Random
House Australia Pty Ltd
Creative Direction by Evi O | Design by Susan Le
Cover and internal photography by Dean Cambray
Styling by Leesa O'Reilly
Typeset in Calluna and Moderat by Post Pre-Press Group,
Brisbane, Australia
Printed and bound in China by RR Donnelley.

 A catalogue record for this
book is available from the
National Library of Australia

ISBN 978 0 14378 913 0

penguin.com.au